T0165328

Goin' to
Weather

Sailing Through a Life of Headwinds

SALLY BOND

Archway Publishing books may be ordered through booksellers or by contacting:

Archway Publishing
1663 Liberty Drive
Bloomington, IN 47403
www.archwaypublishing.com
1-(888)-242-5904

The names of personal friends I talk about in my book
have been changed to protect their identity.

ISBN: 978-1-4808-0587-3 (sc)
ISBN: 978-1-4808-0706-8 (e)

Library of Congress Control Number: 2014906786

Printed in the United States of America

Archway Publishing rev. date: 06/18/2014

To my husband, Walt Bond, for his encouragement
and comprehensive expertise.

To my son, Bob Boyes, for his poignant
and constructive comments.

These two people have given me the support
and patience needed to write this book.
I love them both with all my heart.

Contents

Preface

My personal journey through life and the history of events transpiring within this era are the focus of *Goin' To Weather.*

I was born in the Great Depression. The austerity it provoked and World War II impacted my early years. Marriage, raising two sons, heartbreak, and the joy of sailing brought tears, as well as jubilant celebration. Presidential decisions have affected all our lives, the repercussions of which are part of my story.

The terminology invoked in the title *Goin' to Weather* is derived from a sailing term denoting a boat captain and crew driving a racing sailboat hard, fast, and efficiently into a headwind. Discipline is required to push the limit, to face challenges head-on, while keeping a critical eye on pursuing the ultimate objective.

Goin' to weather is staying on course, while crashing through fierce waves. This term translates into dealing with life's stumbles, tragedies, and successes—while achieving hard-fought goals along a sometimes tumultuous pathway.

As in trudging through life, there are complicated variables in sailboat racing, such as keeping track of the competition and making sure another boat does not sail between you and the wind (blocking your ability to maximize speed). Ocean currents are strong and can take a boat off course. Racing sailors track the direction of currents as vehemently as they do wind direction and strength.

Changing weather patterns alter the dynamics of a race. During rainsqualls, wind velocity goes from zero to fierce gusts. Boat crews quickly dive into their duffel bags down below to grab foul-weather gear and scurry back up on deck. A smaller headsail is hoisted to keep the boat as upright as possible. The wind is strong and waves build. Battling the elements takes precedence over beating the competition.

On the weather leg of a race, the sail trimmer clutches a winch handle, grinding a line around the winch, bringing the sail taut against the stays. Spare crew sit far out on the rail, earning the term *rail meat*. The boat is hard on the wind—the ride rough and wet. Other boats crisscross ahead and behind, all climbing to weather. One last tack sets the boat up for rounding the weather mark.

At this point, competing boats converge upon each other, fighting for the advantage of getting to the mark first. Boat crews are ready to let out sails and raise the spinnaker as soon as the buoy is cleared. The helmsman squeezes the boat around the anchored buoy and, if lucky, misses hitting it—a rerounding is required if you hit the buoy. Mass confusion prevails.

Once around the weather mark, the downwind ride begins. The mainsheet is relaxed as the spinnaker sail is raised to the top of the mast. When the spinnaker fills, the boat leaps forward, surfing the waves and blasting toward home. Sailing off the wind is about speed! Jackets are thrown below and drinks and sandwiches are wolfed down. The helmsman steers a straight course for the finish line, while the crew pumps the main and trims the spinnaker to make the boat obtain maximum speed. Everyone on the boat is focused on treading lightly across the deck to adjust sails, keeping the boat steady.

Sailboat captains must be skillful, knowledgeable, and competent leaders, able to make swift and unhesitating decisions under harrowing conditions. Taking control in extreme conditions entails being strong-willed and unflinching when things go wrong and having patience and perseverance to correct mistakes.

The above analogy has created the basis of my philosophy. It embodies steering a course that will attain preset goals. Variables constantly occur, making it imperative to keep focused on the attainment of winning and achievement, never capitulating along the way.

Preparation is clearly what separates the winners from the losers in life. Realistic comprehension is needed to attain a chosen goal. Education, experience, a strong and resilient mind and body, a good attitude, money, time, focus, and compliance of family and business associates are essential components. The will to achieve and passion for the endeavor are fundamental and absolutely necessary.

Fun and comradeship come into action. Trudging through this gigantic ordeal of life without sharing the light side with close mates would be stressful and overwhelming.

I have stumbled through life, winning a few races and losing a few too. I could have done a better job. With all those stumbles, I'm proud of my achievements.

My story is how I have imperfectly strived to achieve goals and dealt with roadblocks along the way.

The sea is there to challenge.

CHAPTER 1

Depression; Childhood; World War II

Depression in America

Grandpa and Grandma Drake raised nine children in the early part of the twentieth century on a tenant farm in the Midwest. Their children grew up in poverty, but all went to school while helping out on the farm.

My dad served in the marines during the second Nicaraguan Campaign in the late 1920s. He was a sharpshooter. Most of his battalion lost their lives. Pop cut off a buddy's arm that was infected with gangrene.

The Depression had taken hold of our nation in the early 1930s. On November 2, 1932, Franklin D. Roosevelt won the presidency in a landslide victory. Before he was inaugurated, the American banking system shut down.

Mom and Pop were newlyweds. My dad worked ten-hour days six days a week as a diesel mechanic in an automotive garage. Most

|*US Marine Sergeant Bob Lynch*|

everyone was poor. Jobs were scarce, and wages were low. Mom graduated from high school, and my dad had a fourth-grade education. They were quietly married and began life together with a bare minimum of worldly possessions. Both were intelligent, caring, and honest people who continually strived to improve themselves.

Farmers were burning cow manure for fuel. Horses starved, and cows lost their milk. A drought affected the Midwest, causing a giant dust bowl. Depression-era singers sang mournful songs describing the pitiful conditions.

I was born on November 12, 1934, at Mercy Hospital in Council Bluffs, Iowa. The name on the birth certificate is Marilyn Margaret Lynch; however, my dad called me Sally Bug or Sally Doll because I was a little kid. Sally stuck throughout my life. My dad, a veteran, was disappointed my birthday was

|*Bob and Frances Lynch's wedding day photo*|

not on Armistice Day, November 11. To please him, I have always celebrated my birthday on November 11 and 12. My brother, Robert, was born a year and a half before me.

Our young family lived on a small farm in the middle of rural America. Mom cooked on a wood-burning stove, which also provided heat during the harsh Iowa winters. The small dirt road leading up to our house was lined with corn stalks, a vegetable garden, and a chicken coop. The outhouse sat a ways away from the back of the house.

Mom canned tomatoes, corn, green beans, strawberries, apples, rhubarb, and chicken. My brother and I squished tomatoes for canning by stomping on them in a large tub. Mom cut

|Sitting quietly at two years old|

the heads off chickens with a butcher knife. The headless chickens thrashed helplessly in the grass. We chased them down—their bloody necks sometimes stuck in the dirt. The smell of a chicken after being dipped in boiling water stays with you. Feathers could easily be plucked off their bodies after the dunking. Potatoes and onions were stored in a dugout cellar, where they stayed cool in the summertime. I was not allowed to play in the cellar—Mom didn't want her potatoes mixed up with the onions. Milk and churned butter came from our cow, who was gentle and minded Mom when she scolded the animal. We gathered eggs each day from the chicken nests. Noisy roosters woke us every morning.

Our lives were simple, with no refinements. Mom relentlessly told me, "Sally, don't chase the chickens. They won't lay eggs if they are tired."

On occasion, my brother and I played with a couple of young boys who lived down the road. I didn't like them. Little girls are defenseless among a bunch of rascals. Their bullying and threats scared the billy-be-jesus out of me. I learned to suspect any male kid that had threatening tendencies, such as pulling me behind or into a barn. Running away, kicking with all my might, and hiding were my defenses.

Playing with the chickens and making mud pies in our back yard entertained me. My brother chased me a lot, so I learned to run faster than he could.

My parents were completely devoted to one another. Their love of each other is a treasured remembrance. Mom typically prepared a dinner of homemade dumplings or noodles with chicken and vegetables, while rolling out dough for an apple pie. While she labored in the kitchen, Pop enjoyed coming up behind her and putting his muscled arms around Mom's waist, squeezing her breasts in a giant bear hug. I tried not to look.

Mom was a great cook. Pop enthusiastically devoured everything she whipped up in the kitchen. Their love and respect for each other and those around them were positive aspects in my life. Arguments were few. There was too much work to do to worry about mundane trivia.

Luckily, my dad always had a job; however, unemployment in America was over 20 percent. The government stepped in with a much-needed public works program in 1935. Workers hired under this plan built highways, bridges, dams, parks, schools, courthouses, hospitals, the Lincoln Tunnel, La Guardia Airport, Skyline Drive in Virginia, the overseas highway in the Florida Keys, two aircraft carriers, and a light cruiser.

Also, the Social Security Act became law in 1935, financed by a tax of 1 percent on employers with eight or more workers and employee contributions of 1 percent.

My Grandpa Drake, as dirt poor as he always was, never signed up for Social Security. He said he never paid into it, so he didn't deserve to collect it.

Poor wages, long work hours, unsafe working conditions and no job security brought labor unions into existence. My dad never joined a union. He always stood up for management and felt workers should be grateful for their jobs. He stayed at work until the job was finished and never asked to be treated special.

During the first few years of childhood I developed rickets, the disease that deforms skeletal bones because of malnutrition. We either didn't have enough nutrients in our diet, or I ate poorly. Many children developed this destructive disease during the 1930s and early '40s. I was cross-eyed. Looking straight ahead, one eye was visible. The other eye was hidden from view. My first pair of glasses, at age three, helped to bring them together.

When I was five, we moved from our small farm on the outskirts of town to a much nicer home within the city. It was among other houses on a quiet street. This was a transition to urban life. No more farm animals or fields to grow vegetables. A good school was within walking distance. The Heckenorf family lived next door. They had a daughter about my age who became a good friend, but I felt badly that her last name had a cuss word in it.

Our house, along with all the other neighborhood houses, had a basement. The coal furnace took up most of the floor space. My brother and I helped Pop keep the furnace stoked. We had a Victrola phonograph, encased in a tall wooden cabinet, in the corner of the basement. A hand crank played records with titles like: "Three Little Fishes," "Mairzy Doats," and a few Al Jolson tunes. If there was an opportunity, I turned the Victrola crank like crazy so that a full song played before the contraption stopped. Pretending I was a ballerina, I danced and twirled all over the basement to the music.

Before moving to the city I had never seen a swing that wasn't attached to a tree. One of our new neighbors had a metal stand-alone swing set. It looked inviting. I sat myself in the little seat, swinging higher and higher, reaching up to the sky. A boy, up to no good, came up behind me and whacked me over the back of the head with a metal bar while I had my body fully extended. That ended my fun. My skull is still concave from the blow. My parents held a chunk of ice on the back of my head to help reduce the swelling.

Playing with dolls never interested me because that involved being indoors, instead of outdoors. Climbing fences and trees, playing hopscotch and marbles with the neighborhood boys, running through puddles, playing in the mud, and rolling in the snow were the neat things to do. My knees were always skinned up from trying to jump over whatever was in front of me. Mom scolded me often for tearing my dresses and getting them muddy.

Robert and I seldom played together, we had nothing in common, and were distinct opposites. He was quiet-natured, not rough and tumble like me. My parents were too busy to play with me but tried hard to make me mind.

During the first few grades in school I perfected my ability to get the most out of recess and to ignore the lessons my teachers were teaching. My brother, on the other hand, listened to his teachers and did his homework. I didn't like bringing books home from school. My grades were adequate.

I was too young to understand where the world was headed. My parents were interested in current events, but I don't know how much of a worldview they had prior to the war. Their focus was working hard to feed and clothe us.

Events on the World Stage

Our country was beginning to dig itself out of the Depression. It took little notice of what was happening on the other side of the Atlantic. The aggressor in World War I had risen to become the aggressor in another war. Adolf Hitler had dictatorial power in Germany, and Jews were being persecuted by Nazi thugs. The Holocaust had begun.

On March 14, 1938, Hitler motored triumphantly through the city where he lived in lonely poverty as a youth—Vienna Austria. His rampaging army wanted to rule the continent of Europe, including Russia. This news was not in our newspaper or radio headlines. Americans were disinterested in the world around them. We had an isolationist mentality. The military budget was low. A war would be costly. Military involvement in Europe was not considered to be in our best interest because of the collapse of our economy in the Depression.

Jews and other refugees were desperately trying to flee countries in and around Germany and Austria. Their lives were hanging by a thread. During the early 1930s, hundreds of Jewish professors and Jewish physicists were fired from their jobs in Germany and Italy. These scientist refugees came to America—eleven of them to become Nobel Prize winners. President Roosevelt extended visas for German and Austrian citizens living in the United States, including physicist Albert Einstein.

Nuclear fission was first discovered in 1938 at the German Chemistry Institute. The race was on to develop a nuclear bomb among Germany, Japan, the United States, and Russia.

In the early 1940s at Los Alamos, New Mexico, an assemblage of scientific brains the likes of which had never been gathered worked on the design of a bomb that imploded a plutonium sphere in upon itself. [1]

---

[1] I learned more about this project years later. My future husband, Walt Bond, had a close connection with the Manhattan Project. His father, Jack Bond, had a PhD in Physics. Jack worked on the development of the bomb at Los Alamos, under Dr. Robert Oppenheimer, the director of the nuclear bomb program. The War Department took control of the project and code-named it the Manhattan Engineering Project. Walt, his mother and sister lived with his dad in government regulation housing within the well-guarded ultrasecret location during the 1940s.

Only America had the money, material, manpower, natural resources, space, and time necessary to bring an enterprise on the scale of the Manhattan Project to successful completion.

The European theater of war had its tentacles moving toward us across the Atlantic. As disconcerting as this was, a new threat emerged on the Pacific side of our country.

Silent and undetected at sea, several hundred miles northwest of Hawaii, on December 7, 1941, Japanese navy ships were sailing under Japanese Prime Minister Tojo's pennant. The fleet pointed into the wind at dawn to launch their bombers.

The surprise attack had not been detected by American forces stationed on the island. The Japanese air force commander broke radio silence as his planes droned toward their target. "Tora! Tora! Tora!" was his coded message back to the Japanese fleet that their strike on American war ships was about to begin. American sailors on the sinking battleships that were bombed were sitting ducks— over 2,400 of them died.

The US Congress declared war on Japan on December 8, 1941. Hitler was elated that the Japanese had attacked an American military base and felt it was now impossible for the Germans to lose the war in Europe. On December 11, 1941, German Dictator Adolf Hitler and Italian Dictator Benito Mussolini declared war on the United States.

Our family was transfixed in front of the radio as President Roosevelt said, "This day, December 7, 1941, will go down in infamy." No one knew what would happen next. We were scared. However, we had great confidence in our president, government, and military.

Iowa Upbringing

Council Bluff's only movie theater opened up with a news show entitled "The Eyes and Ears of the World Are upon You," with dramatic music, that showed warships pounding through rough seas across the ocean and big deck cannons shooting at Nazi or Jap ships. The movies were usually westerns or comic book serials (I wanted to be like Wonder Woman because she could deflect bullets with her wristbands). Western movies were boring, and serials (except for *Wonder Woman*) were scary. I liked newsreels the best. It cost a nickel to ride the streetcar to downtown Council Bluffs. On Sunday mornings my parents gave me twenty-five cents—ten cents for streetcar fare and fifteen cents for the church collection plate. I usually blew off Sunday school and went to the movie, which cost eleven cents. This left me with four cents to buy candy.

My brother and I took piano lessons while we were both in grade school. Robert did well, learning to do scales and some nice little songs. I didn't like playing the piano and told my teacher, who informed my mom that she was wasting her money on me. That ended my piano lessons and freed me up to play more hopscotch.

Mom had the hard job of making me mind and punishing me for my frequent misbehavior, shaping my values, making me read books and do household chores. I was almost always on my best behavior around my gentle and loving father, because I wanted to please him.

Pop loved to work on diesel engines. He could tell what was wrong with the engine by just listening to it. His employer, the Street Railway Company, provided streetcar and bus transportation to Council Bluffs and Omaha. Pop was foreman of the maintenance garage, in charge of keeping the buses repaired.This was a daunting job, due to the inclement weather in the Midwest. During winter months, the doors of the bus garage were kept closed with bus engines running. Men working down in the pits beneath the buses were easily overcome with deadly carbon monoxide gas. My dad was hospitalized twice, and his lungs were severely scarred from the noxious fumes.

We belonged to the First Baptist Church in downtown Council Bluffs. My folks' priority, if there was any spare time, was fishing. Regular church attendance never happened.

The Baptist Church believes in total immersion baptism. When parishioners understand the word of Jesus Christ, they are baptized. I was ten years old when I stepped into the baptismal water. The preacher held me under for, what I thought, a very long time. My mom said it was because I had so many sins to forgive.

Council Bluffs is, above all, a railroad town. Going to church or to downtown stores on the streetcar meant crossing numerous railroad crossings and waiting for seemingly endless trains to pass.

Life was a mixture of small town activities interrupted by radio broadcasts telling us about a war in foreign countries. It was difficult for me to relate to the reported atrocities being committed. Cruelty to me was my brother hiding my marbles.

World War II

Prior to the 1940s, America was bogged down in the effects of the Depression. We were a mostly rural nation, trying to make it in everyday life struggles. World War II came upon us as just one more weight pushing us toward the abyss.

We grew what we ate, made what we wore, and entertainment meant going for a walk down the road, seeing a movie, or reading books from the library. Our family, friends, and neighbors pinched pennies, didn't waste anything, and used a menthol rub to cure most illnesses. Efficiency ruled, and there were no excuses for not doing assigned chores. Inner toughness was a way of life.

My parents valued family get-togethers. Mom cooked wholesome Sunday and holiday dinners, inviting neighbors or relatives to eat with us. The dining room table was set with a hand-embroidered tablecloth and napkins for those special occasions.

Our black cat ate the rodents. If the cat got in the way of my dad's foot, it got a swift kick. Early in the morning, if Pop thought he was alone in the kitchen, he tickled the cat under its chin with his shoe. I don't remember my dad ever touching the cat we called Churchill (it had a white V for victory marking on its chest).

The international world stage was a long way from our little
Iowa town. My favorite subject in school was history. Teachers tried
to bring world events to us, explaining what countries our troops
were fighting against and what countries were helping us.
Invention of lightweight material improved American aircraft
manufacturers' ability to build planes that were competitive with the
enemy's. A multitude of scientific innovations created during wartime
eventually reshaped America into the world's most powerful nation.

Germany and Japan both hoped for a short war because of the
tremendous industrial power of America.

The war rescued our economy from the Depression. Unused
factories were converted into producers of war machines. The
large unemployed labor force went to work in these factories.
Sixteen million Americans joined the military. Income tax rates on
corporations were raised and withholding taxes were deducted from
workers' paychecks to foot the war bill. War spending skyrocketed
from $3.6 billion in 1940 to $93.4 billion in 1944.

America sent troops into the Atlantic theater. American/British
war efforts in North Africa against the Germans were going poorly
until Eisenhower appointed General George Patton as commander
of the operation. Slowly, the tide began to turn in the Allies' favor.[2]

Life, for us, did not change dramatically during the war. Pop's
job was secure because there was a skilled labor shortage. He was
needed on the home front.

---

2   General Patton trained his troops for desert warfare in our backyard.
    The California mountains and washes that surround the area around the
    Colorado River, where we have a vacation home, were alive with tanks,
    airplanes, and soldiers in the early 1940s. Old bullet shells are scattered
    in the sand. There is a block of cement that was used as a bombing site
    out in the middle of a large wash. Now, it is a favorite meeting place
    for a beer break when we are riding through this desert landscape on
    motorcycles or dunebuggies. A friend of ours painted a tropical scene
    on the bare and chipped piece of cold cement.

My uncles Warren Drake and Bud Hines were drafted into the army, and cousins Ralph, Chuck, and Bobby Smith enlisted in the navy.

|Grandma and Grandpa Drake escorted Uncle Warren to the Council Bluffs, Iowa, train station. He was ready for deployment to his regiment.|

Many houses in our little town displayed a red white and blue banner with embroidered stars in their windows, signifying the sons or fathers in that family that were fighting in the war or that had been killed in action. None of my relatives were killed or captured during the war.

History lessons at school were watered down. We were not told of the horrors of war, only what battles were won. Nothing was said of the extermination of Jews, their misery or persecution. Christianity was the accepted religion throughout the Midwest. Therefore, Jews were not in our Christian mindset.

To save fabrics, the War Department banned double-breasted suits, trouser cuffs, patch pockets, pleated skirts, and hemlines went up! New private home construction was restricted, and the manufacture of automobiles was prohibited. Meat, butter, flour, coffee, and sugar were rationed. Mom and I took ration coupons to the store to buy the monthly allotment of these scarce items. Tires and gasoline were also rationed. Silk stockings were no longer made, and all chocolate candy went to the troops.

The war effort inspired everyone to sacrifice and not complain. America was at her best, although the cost in lives was great. We stood together as a proud nation. My school buddies and I did whatever our teachers asked of us, such as saving tin foil from gum wrappers for the war effort. We didn't waste chalk, pencils, or paper.

Mom and Pop frequented the Veterans of Foreign Wars Club in Omaha, where they could drink a beer with other veterans and exchange war news.

Throughout the war, President Roosevelt continued his fireside chats. Our family listened intently to his radio addresses giving us status reports on the war. His reassuring words told us America and its allies would prevail. There was

|My brother Robert (holding our cat named Churchill) and I|

no partisan bickering during this time of crises. We stood together against Hitler, Mussolini and Hirohito!

No one took a vacation. We did not have a car; we took the public streetcar everywhere, or walked. Our local grocery store was about six blocks away. Residential roads were not paved. I ice skated to the store in between the ruts in the road in the winter and ran there in the summer, splashing through road puddles along the way. Mom sewed our clothes and patched them when they needed it.

I was too young to be in World War II but always dreamed of being a Wave in the Navy Corps because of a burning desire to see the ocean. I had seen the mighty ocean in newsreels and was positive that I would someday witness its power and beauty.

As D-Day approached (June 6, 1944) the Axis outnumbered the Allied troops because every able-bodied man and boy was conscripted into the German military. However, German manpower and machinery were exhausted. Fresh American manpower and modern machinery ground the Germans down.

Nearly four million American troops in England were prepared and waiting for the D-Day invasion. The Brits quipped, "The Yanks are overpaid, oversexed, and over here." The Yanks replied, "The Brit's are underpaid, undersexed, and under Eisenhower."

In all, 291,557 Americans were killed in action in World War II. Dramatic advances in medical science, among them penicillin and blood transfusions, saved thousands of lives. Soldiers with battle fatigue were not coddled. They kept on fighting. My Uncle Bud did his best for the troops. His job was to guard the whisky inside of an American military camp somewhere in France. He told us he sat on top of the bunker where the whisky was housed, his rifle nearby.

Hitler was becoming obstinate with his military leaders. A colonel in the German army attempted to kill Hitler with a bomb, but Hitler survived to launch uncontrolled fury on his military leaders. Irrational decisions by Hitler exacerbated the hopelessness of further attacks against the far superior Allied invasion force. Two of Hitler's top generals committed suicide.

General Eisenhower made a difficult and controversial decision to end the war quickly by demoralizing the German citizenry. An air attack on Berlin and Dresden in February, 1945, killed sixty-five thousand civilians. The cities were burned and destroyed.

By April, American troops reached the banks of the Elbe River, the agreed boundary between the Soviet and Western zones of occupation. The Red Army proceeded to take Berlin.

Blacks and women learned the power of education through their imposed segregation in the military during the war. White male rule of the business and political world was about to be challenged. However, it happened slowly. Accepted values during the 1940s dictated that leaders of our country be white, Protestant, and male. Few questioned this philosophy or stepped out of their paradigm. My mom and all the other moms I knew stayed home and raised their children, while the fathers brought home the bacon. Higher education was reserved for the breadwinners.

In an effort to have the postwar economy absorb the men in uniform, Congress unanimously passed the GI Bill of Rights in June 1944. Vocational training, higher education, housing, medical benefits while in school, and low interest rates to buy homes and start businesses were assured for veterans. This bill forever changed America by empowering the veterans through education and training. Higher productivity, along with a better-educated workforce, brought achievement and affluence to Americans.

This was the right thing to do. Our World War II veterans came home with their heads held high, full of energy to get an education, start a family, and build a home for themselves and their loved ones. The draft worked during a time of crises for the United States. America was grateful to those that served our nation.

As the presidential election neared in 1944, Roosevelt's health was failing. This tired and strained man had brought us to the brink of peace. He decided to make a run for president for an unprecedented fourth term. My parents thought it was time for someone fresh to take over presidential duties, but the majority of the country disagreed.

Harry S. Truman was chosen as the vice presidential nominee. He had a moderate stance and down-to-earth philosophy. His education stopped after high school. Truman achieved the rank of captain in World War I.

Americans were isolated from the atrocities of the war, due to government censorship ("Loose lips sink ships"). The Holocaust of Jews was now being reported. Americans knew Jews were smart and self-sufficient. They also were among America's preeminent bankers, educators. and scientists. Hitler's belief that the arian race was superior to any other race was nonsenceical. His desire to destroy the Jewish race was pure evil.

Roosevelt's inaugural address on January 20, 1945, was short. We listened to it on the radio. The newspapers reported that he appeared gravely ill. Even so, he sailed across the Atlantic, where he rendezvoused with Prime Minister Winston Churchill, then he and Churchill flew to Yalta to meet with the Soviet Union's General Secretary, Joseph Stalin.

Issues discussed during this momentous gathering of world leaders included membership rules for the newly formed United Nations organization, including the fate of Eastern Europe and the treatment of a defeated Germany.

The trip to Yalta must have been excruciatingly difficult for Roosevelt, who was not only a sick man but paralyzed from the waist down, due to polio. I always thought of Roosevelt as an old man, but not handicapped. The press did a magnificent job of covering up his paralysis.

Stalin was strong and demanding at the conference. Roosevelt was vague and unsure of himself. He gave in to Stalin's demands on UN voting rights, giving the Soviets two extra vetoes in the General Assembly. No decision was made about postwar Germany. Roosevelt caved on Stalin's demands to annex the northerly islands off Japan and control over the Manchurian railroad (opening the door for Communist takeover of China). Churchill had little impact at the conference.

President Roosevelt died April 12, 1945, of a cerebral hemorrhage at his retreat in Georgia. Harry S. Truman was sworn in four hours later in the cabinet room of the White House.

Our nation went into mourning. A train carried Roosevelt's body back to Washington. Millions of people lined the tracks along the way, paying homage to the man who had done so much for America's poor and for his leadership in World War II. We heard his funeral on the radio, and I saw a newsreel of the funeral at the movie theater. I, along with most everyone else in the theater, cried, knowing that we had not only lost a true leader but that his voice was now silenced. The Roosevelt era was over.

Benito Mussolini was assassinated on April 28, 1945, by Italian citizens who were fighting against the Axis. On April 30, Adolf Hitler shot himself in his bunker in West Berlin. Communist troops were fighting the Germans for Berlin, the Nazi capital. Germany's unconditional surrender came a week later, ending the war in Europe.

I was eleven years old and felt the joyful mood of my parents and relatives. Women were talking about the end of ration stamps and the ability to again buy silk stockings. Men knew wartime restrictions would end. Maybe we could buy a car.

Before this could happen, America needed to win the Pacific war.

Japanese soldiers were taught not to surrender. Their captives were treated as cowards, not due any respect. American POWs were beaten, tortured, starved, and killed with no regard for human decency.

The last two battles in the Pacific, Iwo Jima and Okinawa, were fiercely fought. Tremendous courage was shown. On a single day, five marines earned the Congressional Metal of Honor. Squadrons of Japanese suicide planes pelted American ships in kamikaze dives. Seventy thousand Japanese soldiers, one hundred thousand civilians, and 12,600 American servicemen were killed in the fierce battles for these two islands.

Truman was working with his military advisers on a plan to invade Japan. Knowing that the Japanese would fight to the death and not be taken captive, it was feared the loss of lives from an invasion would be a costly way to go.

The decision to use the atomic bomb was lightly debated among politicians and military advisers. The full devastating impact of dropping a bomb that was the most powerful device ever conceived, with radiation consequences, was not taken into consideration. Everyone, from Truman on down, agreed the bomb should be used to push the Japanese into submission. They all knew this would end the war.

Air Force Colonel Paul Tibbits handpicked B-29 no. 82 off the Martin Corporation's bomber production line in Omaha. He renamed it after his mother, Enola Gay. On August 6, 1945, Tibbits flew the Enola Gay from the Mariana Islands to Hiroshima and dropped an atomic bomb.

The Japanese people were stunned. However, their scientists did not think it possible for another bomb to be dropped because they felt the Americans could not possibly have enough radioactive material to produce more bombs. There was no sign of surrender. On August 9 another nuclear bomb was dropped, on Nagasaki. This was the end of Japanese aggression.

The headlines in newspapers were of the terrific news that the Japs were going to surrender. We thought little about the devastation the bombs created. Our thoughts were for the American soldiers coming home because they had won the war. Excitement grew to a fever pitch, and everyone celebrated—my classmates and I in school, and Mom and Pop went to the VFW Hall in Omaha to have a victory drink with other veterans. It was a time to gather around the radio and listen to the earth-shaking news that World War II was over!

For most of my young life, we had been at war with Germany and Japan. I didn't know what it was like to not need ration stamps to buy groceries. The fear that a relative might be killed or captured by the enemy had been a constant for most of our citizens.

Emperor Hirohito prepared a surrender announcement declaring that Japan's war with the United States had ended. On September 2, 1945, the battleship *Missouri* was anchored in Tokyo Bay for the signing of the surrender documents. The flagstaff atop the battleship flew the forty-eight-star flag that had flown over the Capitol Dome on December 7, 1941. Japanese officials signed the documents, and then General Douglas MacArthur, along with Admirals Chester

Nimitz and William Halsey, signed for the Americans. American sailors, and other servicemen who were crowded around the deck, stood at attention. A movie theater newsreel brought this solemn ceremony into view for us. I thought the tall-hatted Japanese officials looked as though they wanted to commit harakiri.

Life changed all at once. Parades were held for returning veterans in every city. It was as if a heavy fog had been lifted off our country, and a euphoria embraced us all. Everyone was relieved and couldn't wait to get started on a new and productive life.

In the early 1940s, our next-door neighbors started to build a home on their lot. National building restrictions prevented further construction. Their basement was completed just as the war broke out. For the next five years they were limited to life in their underground home. As soon as the war ended and building materials again came on the market, neighbors pitched in to help them build their above-ground dream house. My friends and I made wooden airplanes out of the leftover scrap wood and nails. I strutted around the work site in my new white baton boots, throwing my baton high in the air and catching it, while pretending I was leading a parade.

Our family was just as giddy as the rest of the nation. No more restrictions on food or gas, so we could go on vacation!

I was still a kid in grade school and less appreciative of the strains and hardships the war caused. However, it was easy to take advantage of the perks that started coming our family's way. Pop bought a car,

|My dad and I|

and I got a used bicycle. Mom didn't have to paint lines up the back of her legs to look like she was wearing silk stockings. My brother could buy components for his radio listening devices. He had wires strung all over his attic bedroom that allowed him to get static from faraway places.

|Mom|

Mom was a beautiful woman. Her red hair was always piled high on her head. She delighted in dressing up to go out on the town with Pop. They made a handsome couple. My brother and I rode with Mom and Pop in our car to my aunts and uncles, or to our friends' houses to have dinner. I do not remember ever going to a restaurant.

America had a president from Missouri. Midwesterners were delighted and proud to have a person familiar with hometown values and upbringing in the White House.

Peace

Harry "the buck stops here" Truman had only been FDR's vice president eighty-three days when he was sworn into office as president. He jumped from the frying pan into the fire by dropping the world's first nuclear device on Japan during the first days of his presidency.

The United States started cranking out goods and materials for export to Europe, which had to rebuild its war-torn economies. The European's needed food, clothing, medical supplies, and building materials.

American citizens were gleeful and ready to bring normalcy back to their lives. We all loved Truman because we had confidence in his ability to get us back on track, and we thought he was honest. During the Second World War, it was difficult to have children, since most young fathers were fighting abroad. Now that the war was over and the economy was booming, the baby boom generation was about to be created.[3]

The Truman administration created the Marshall Plan, which helped feed Europe's starving and aided their devastated economies. Bombers flew to Germany, not laden with bombs, but with food and clothing. A highway in the sky was established by the tireless efforts of World War II pilots, bringing relief to the masses as quickly as possible. The German people were taken aback by our generosity.

Truman was criticized for not invading China. War hawks had their sights set on the annihilation of Communism. Truman was also criticized for unleashing the atomic bomb on Japan, killing or severely injuring hundreds of thousands of civilians.

I felt that President Truman had high standards and did what was best for the country. He was caught in a catch-22—damned if he didn't end the war quickly and damned if his decision to use the bomb was seen as a ghastly mistake.

As schoolchildren, we continued to save for war bonds, filling the cardboard cutout slots with twenty-five-cent pieces. Our school teachers helped us with the process of purchasing a bond. Children were taught the importance of saving and the responsibility of all Americans to help pay for the war.

My parents expected my brother and me to save money, do chores and not expect payment, and to get odd jobs that paid for nonessentials, such as a bicycle or roller skates. The value and scarcity of money was pounded into our heads.

---

3   My husband, Walt, was in the nascent stage of this worldwide phenomenon.

While Truman was president, he came to Omaha to march in a military parade. This was a special occasion. Mom and I decided to attend the parade. We put a pot of beans on the stove to cook for dinner, and then walked to the streetcar stop, four blocks away. The streetcar crossed the bridge over the wide Missouri River, taking us from Council Bluffs to Omaha.

It was a bright, sunny day, and we were going to see a president of the United States in person. We stood on the corner of a busy downtown thoroughfare as President Truman walked by. He was a short guy and had a brisk stride. His hat was in his hand. The president waved to us and other spectators, while marching in time with music played by a military band.

We had big self-satisfied smiles on our faces as we rode the streetcar back across the Missouri River late in the afternoon. When we stepped off the streetcar at our stop, the grocery store owner across the street yelled out at Mom, "Hey, lady, a fire truck was at your house today." Something had caught on fire. Mom and I picked up our feet and ran home.

We smelled smoke but didn't see any evidence of fire. The pot of beans that was supposed to be dinner had burned up and the whole house was a smoky mess. In our haste to leave the house we forgot to turn the fire down to a simmer. The papered walls of the kitchen, dining room, and living room had heavy black soot on them. For the next few weeks our family was involved in rolling a pink paste over the walls, taking the soot off, little by little. I can still recall the smell of both the pink glop and the smoke smell that permeated the wallpaper.

Family

I grew up in the Midwest and never traveled away from it until after I graduated from high school. This restricted a more worldly view, especially in a family which was largely uneducated. However, my parents were inquisitive and imaginative. They were curious about travel and dreamed about a move to California, where the climate was warm. Wanderlust was in their blood, and in mine.

We had a close relationship with Mom's parents and her nine married brothers and sisters during the 1930s and '40s. Holiday gatherings were with her relatives. We lived less than one hundred miles from each other, some as close as down the street.

The Zephyr train carried my brother and me to Grandpa and Grandma Drake's farm. Numerous cousins and I romped around together. Uncle Warren was my grandparents' youngest child and my favorite uncle. He allowed my cousin Joan and I to hang onto his legs while he pulled us up and down through the cornfields as he shucked the ears of corn.

Mom's family was of average intelligence; none of them went to college. They were good and honest people. Most did not stray out of the Midwest. They didn't gripe about their hardships, but family gossip reigned supreme. When they gathered together on holidays or special occasions, Mom's sisters all vied for telling the biggest whopper about each other, and then laughed their heads off.

The July Fourth annual picnic was a highlight. Grandpa played his fiddle and danced a little jig while we all clapped and sang. Grandma brought homemade berry pies from fruit she picked from her trees and garden; my aunts brought fried chicken and side dishes that made your gut burst because you just could not stop eating. My cousins and I raced around the park and did somersaults and cartwheels.

Grandma was short and fat. She waddled like a duck. Her feet and hands were deformed from arthritis, and I remember she always cut the toes out of her shoes so it didn't hurt so much to walk. My feet and hands have the same deformity, so holes and slits need to be cut in my shoes to accommodate my wayward toes.

Grandpa was tall and thin. He looked a bit like Abraham Lincoln. He was a staunch Republican. My uncles and my dad had political discussions with Grandpa, and as I remember, there was lots of shouting and thumping on the table.

Farming was Grandma and Grandpa Drake's livelihood. They lived simply, without a furnace, refrigeration, or plumbing. Light bulbs were hanging from the ceiling of their house—no wall switches. I always thought of them as "Mutt and Jeff" because they were so different in stature. Their hard life never abated.

My dad had seven brothers and sisters. His father died before I was born. Pop never talked about him and avoided talking about his mother, who we didn't visit very often.

Aunt Grace, my dad's sister, was married to Ralph Smith, an obnoxious alcoholic. They had three wonderful boys, whom I idolized. After making it through the war, two died of disease as young adults. Everything in the Lynch family was so hush-hush that I never heard what the disease was that killed them.

I had one cousin on my dad's side, Sue, who I grew up and played with. There were few get-togethers with my dad's relatives because they were quieter and more restrained than my mom's side of the family. I had a good time with my mom's relatives, but, as a youngster, I never became close with anyone on my dad's side, except for Sue.

Every time I saw my Grandma Lynch she was bedridden, due to arthritis. She was a small person and not cheery. I never saw her walk.

Pop was a breakaway from his family. I believe that my mom's gusto for life complemented my dad's quiet behavior. Both were happy and content throughout their lives.

CHAPTER 2

Growing Up; Postwar; California

Postwar Midwest

With the end of rationing and restrictions on buying food, clothing, cars, and building materials, our attention was directed toward making a better life in a newly revitalized economy.

If my parents had extra money, they never spread the word to me. We still walked everywhere or rode a streetcar, except on special occasions when my dad drove us in the family car.

The world was opening up to us through a new electronic marvel—television. Wrestling matches and the Milton Berle Show were the TV programs broadcast ad nauseam. My friend Dotty had the first television in our neighborhood. This was a great tool to get boys over to her house. What fun we had, making peanut butter and jelly sandwiches and sitting in front of the TV with a sandwich and a glass of milk and boys all around us. Dotty and I were in charge.

Our family's first TV set was slow in coming because of cost.

When it came, the tiny six-inch green screen was enclosed in a large maple cabinet. The picture was fuzzy, and the sound was tinny.

Health problems plagued me as a child. I wanted to be supergirl, but my body was fragile and rebelled against being hammered all the time. I wanted to be an acrobat, ballet and tap dancer, ice skater, and baton twirler. Rheumatic fever took hold of my body in grade school. My knees were stiff and swollen, making it difficult to walk, and I had horrific headaches in the back of my head. I was usually the smallest kid in my school class, and skinny besides. These maladies, along with not studying in school, took their toll. About the time I went into sixth grade, my health improved, and I was back to running everywhere I went.

The local Congregational Church held Boy Scout and Girl Scout meetings and social events in their basement. My girlfriends and I delighted in peeping in the windows, watching the boys participate in scouting awards programs. While the boys were busy with the ceremony, we girls were busy letting the air out of their bicycle tires.

Dinners were held in the church basement, sometimes serving one of my favorite meals—chili! I wolfed down several bowls, hoping to put a pound or two of weight on. No matter how much I ate, I was still a scrawny kid. One of my chunky girlfriends wished she could give me a little of her fat. Friends came up with my nickname, "lunch bucket," derived from my last name, Lynch, and for all the food I endlessly devoured.

Ice skating and roller skating, playing football, swimming, and riding a bike were my passions. Tarzan and Esther Williams movies were all the rage. I thought I swam just like Esther Williams and could swing through the trees like Tarzan. In the summer I picked apples off our backyard trees and sold them to neighborhood ladies so I could buy a season pass to the local swimming pool. The pool lifeguards yelled at me a lot because they thought I was too little to dive off the high diving board.

Climbing trees and jumping from them was fun for me, but it

was my mom who took the splinters out of my hands and rear end and patched my torn clothes.

As a summer pastime, my friends and I rode our bicycles down to the Missouri River to cool off. We did cartwheels along the shoreline and took turns to see who could sink the farthest into the quicksand before being sucked under.

During the winter we ice skated on a nearby lake and played crack the whip. Being the smallest kid in the whip line, I was usually on the end because I flew farther across the ice. This landed me in snowbanks, or sometimes I flew across the ice and into other skaters.

After the war ended, the big event of the year for our family was my dad's two-week summer vacation. He drove us north through Minnesota, crossing the border town of International Falls, where a larger than life statue of Paul Bunyan holding an ax was a photo stop. Just north of there is Lake of the Woods National Park in Kenora, Canada. This area has pristine lakes surrounded by Canadian pines. The large granite rock formations along the lake made excellent diving platforms for me and my pals. My parents spent the entire day on the lake, pulling in fish after fish. They caught enough fish every day to have fried fish, rolled in cornmeal, for breakfast, along with fresh fried potatoes, cold fish for lunch, and more fried fish for supper.

Mom and Pop rented a cabin that was built out over the lake, next to a rickety bridge. There was a trapdoor in their bedroom that opened up into the lake. Mom could set her hook while in bed (I don't know if she ever did this).

Eye Surgery

When I was twelve, I went to a summer church camp on the Iowa River. I have no remembrance of Bible lessons.

I dove off a swinging footbridge that went from one side of the lake to the other. It was at least thirty feet off the water. Twice I got my head stuck in the lake bottom after doing a perfect dive off the bridge. I played games, roasted marshmallows, and told scary ghost stories around a campfire at night with my camp mates. The counselors tried their best to instill the teachings of Jesus into our hearts and souls.

When I returned home from camp, my mom and dad gave me the greatest gift I could imagine. They had scheduled me for eye surgery to correct and straighten my horribly crossed eyes at a hospital in Omaha. Ceaseless teasing from my so-called friends about being cross-eyed would stop.

After the surgery, I was wheeled back to the hospital ward. I could not see because my eyes were bandaged, and I couldn't move my arms or legs. The hospital staff had put me into a straitjacket because I was violent (the same thing had happened when I had my tonsils out). My body fought the effects of ether anesthesia. It took several doctors and nurses to hold me down and stop me from ripping the bandages off my eyes. When I was cognizant, the straitjacket was removed, but restraints were put on my arms so I couldn't reach my eyes.

Five days later, the doctor took off the eye bandages. I looked out the window and saw two identical gardens in the lawn below, instead of one. My eyes were straight, but I saw double (still do). Today, there is a procedure to correct the problem, but I am accustomed to this aberration.

About fifteen other kids were in the hospital ward I was in. Most of them were having surgery for a cleft palate. Some had polio. A couple of iron lung machines were across the hall. The children in them looked ghastly.

After being released from the hospital, Mom, Pop, and my brother stopped by my aunt Bonnie and uncle Cy's house to have dinner. A park across the street had a big swing that I immediately spotted. I ran over to it and was swinging higher and higher. My parents spotted me and raced out of the house and through the park to tell me I wasn't supposed to bounce around or do anything active for a few weeks. I hated sitting quietly.

A week later, Mom took me to the doctor to get the stitches taken out of my eyes. The doctor cut the stitches loose and walked away. I thought he was finished, so I got up and walked into the waiting room. There were screams from other patients because blood was streaming down my face. I was quickly led back into the examination room by the nurses so Dr. Gifford could finish his work of cutting the stitches out of my eyes.

High School

Studying subjects taught in high school was not a high priority for me, thereby wasting my opportunity to gain self-confidence through education. My brother and I had to walk a long way to school. I found it was hard to carry books and throw snowballs. My books stayed in the school locker.

I played the violin in the school orchestra, and even performed in a couple of concerts (my mom said she didn't know which squeaked more, the cotton she had put in the bodice of my formal to give me a little shape or the violin I was trying to play).

My body matured slowly. I was sixteen before I started to menstruate, and I had not developed breasts before this auspicious occurrence. Mom celebrated when *it* happened. She had great hopes of me growing out of my tomboy stage.

College was not even a glimmer in my head. I didn't feel I was smart enough, so I didn't take college prep courses. At that time in my life, I knew nothing about setting goals, other than I wanted to graduate from high school, find a clerical job, choose a good husband, and have babies. This is what all my girlfriends aspired to. I didn't have any erudite role models. My female peers were stuck in the same rut I was in. Few girls were encouraged to continue their education after high school. I thought an engineer drove trains.

A desire to push myself to the limit and the discipline to accomplish significant goals came much later in life. However, my parents' moral standards were a guiding light. They always taught my brother and me to be responsible for ourselves. I tried to not burden Mom and Pop with anything I thought I could handle. In retrospect, I should have asked them questions and been more communicative about my feelings of inadequacy. This could have helped me mature.

In my last year of high school, my parents sold our home in Council Bluffs, and we moved to Omaha. I changed high schools, which caused me grief because I was losing all the friends I grew up with in Council Bluffs and enrolling in a monstrous high school in Omaha, where I didn't know anyone.

To help support the cost of my leisure activities and meet new friends, I got a job in a local drugstore as a soda jerk. I learned to smoke there. This job was for me! I built malts, shakes, sodas, and ice-cream cones for the boys as they sat on swivel chairs watching me hop around my little kingdom.

During my last semester of high school I worked part-time at Mutual of Omaha, a large insurance company. It paid thirty cents an hour, and I typed zillions of insurance policies.

The week prior to graduation from high school, the entire senior class was bused to a lodge on the outskirts of Omaha for a three-day celebration. We were housed in gender-segregated barracks-type buildings. There was also a sandpit (man-made) lake, with a tall diving platform and a tree swing in the middle of the lake. The sun was blazing, and our pale bodies were not ready for its intensity.

I had become friends with most of my graduating class and was enjoying the outing. Diving off the high platform diving board was exhilarating. A bunch of us swam out to the tree swing and climbed the ladder to the top, where a long rope hung down toward the water below. I grabbed the knots in the rope and propelled myself off the ladder structure. I tried hard to swing higher and higher before dropping into the water. When I let go of the rope I heard yelling about snakes in the water. Looking down, I saw a nest of cottonmouth snakes right below me. I took a deep breath and pointed my toes, diving way below the surface, then swam underwater like crazy toward the diving platform at the edge of the lake. I chipped my tooth getting out of the water, but the snakes had not caught me. The lake was cleared. After three days of fun in the sun, our sunburned bodies were bused back to Omaha. I graduated in June 1952. We wore wool gowns to the ceremony, which made our peeling skin feel like it was on fire.

Our graduation dance was a formal affair. The guy who asked me to the dance was a handsome hunk and looked just like Rock Hudson! He bought me a corsage. We held hands and danced, and he kissed me lightly on the mouth when he took me home, upholding the traditional values learned growing up in the Midwest.

We knew sex was taboo. Girls saved themselves for their white knight in shining armor. Boys were shy and awkward. Adults were all married or widowed. I didn't know anyone who was divorced, and I certainly had never heard of a woman having a child out of wedlock.

Korean War

Halfway around the world, the chaos of war reared its ugly head for the second time in my life. On June 25, 1950, North Korean Communist forces attacked South Korea.

The United Nations Security Council named the United States to direct the military operations, and President Truman ordered the general of the army, Douglas MacArthur, to repel the invasion. Truman later fired MacArthur, who wanted to carry the war into China.

Dwight D. Eisenhower was elected president in 1952. He brought to the presidency his prestige as commanding general of the victorious US forces in Europe during World War II.

The Korean War roared on. Troops from other countries poured into the region. In this "forgotten war" 33,741 US servicemen lost their lives.[4]

On July 27, 1953, an armistice was signed at Panmunjom, South Korea. The fighting ended. Each side pulled back two thousand meters from the demilitarized zone. A cease-fire was agreed to at the forty-ninth parallel. So many soldiers and civilians were killed and maimed. South Korea was free, but the price of the Korean War was staggering, and the result was incomplete. Today, North Korea is an extremely repressive Communist state with nuclear bomb capabilities. South Korea is a democratic republic. It's citizenry is well educated and their economy grows at a rapid rate.

My brother joined the air force just as the Korean War was winding down. His world changed when his first duty of service was in Japan. Robert met a young Japanese girl. They were married in Japan. I wrote him a scathing letter, telling him of my displeasure of him marrying someone of Japanese heritage. I had no right to condemn their marriage. When Robert brought his bride back to the States after he was discharged, I found they had a happy marriage. I apologized to them both for my obnoxious letter. They forgave me and we became friends.

After the Korean War ended, Eisenhower turned America toward domestic issues. An interstate highway system was designed and built. It would not only tie the East Coast to the West Coast for peacetime travel and shipping, Eisenhower also recognized it would

---

4   My first husband, Bill, was just out of high school when he enlisted in the military. He served aboard a navy destroyer between 1951 and 1952. The ship patrolled the South China Sea in search of enemy combatants. Heavy action eluded them, but Bill came home with stories of rough seas that tossed their destroyer around like a toy.

also provide transportation routes for troops and military supplies in case of foreign invasion.

In the US boom of the 1950s and early '60s, refrigerators, cars, televisions, and washing machines were produced in the millions and sold to a hungry citizenry. It was a great time to be a young adult. New inventions and improvements in existing technology were prolific. America held itself to high standards and morals. We respected our leaders as they took us through a period of peace and prosperity.

America was making great strides toward having modern conveniences and higher living standards, while Eisenhower emphasized a balanced budget and peaceful solutions to international crises.

The Cold War had its beginnings after Germany was split into Communist East Germany and a democratic West Germany. The Potsdam Conference agreement confirmed the partition of Berlin among Allies. Faced with strained relations between the Soviet Union and the United States, Eisenhower worked tirelessly to end hostilities. Both countries had developed hydrogen bombs. Our family, along with most other citizens, were not overly concerned about a foreign Cold War. We were caught up in how new innovations would change our world for the better.

Move to California

In the early 1950s my father developed ulcers because of his demanding job. It was because of this that Mom and Pop finally decided it was time to move out of the cold and snowy winters of the Iowa/Nebraska plains.

Mom sold our house, and Pop quit his job. We gave away all of our worldly possessions, except for our clothes. After getting settled in our new home, new products on the market would replace our old worn out household goods.

Southern California, here we come! It held the promise of a new job for Pop. As 1953 began, in the middle of a fierce winter storm, we piled into the family Studebaker and drove to the West Coast. None of us had been west of Nebraska. We were stacked to the gills. Mom's pocketbook held the family finances. Pop's tool chest was in the trunk of the car. In the backseat, my brother and I perched ourselves on top of our family clothing, reading comic books for most of the trip. I do remember stopping at the Grand Canyon and the Petrified Forest National Parks along the way.

My parents were following their dream of moving west, a life-changing adventure. Their apprehensions must have been enormous. My brother and I were ignorant in our understanding of what challenges Mom and Pop faced.

We arrived at the Long Beach home of my dad's brother, Cy, and his wife, Bonnie, and daughter, Sue, in the middle of January. I was excited to be in the proximity of the ocean. The day after our arrival, my goal of seeing the Pacific Ocean was fulfilled. It was a blustery winter day, cold and windy. My Uncle Cy took us sightseeing and drove us to the beach. I ran from the car and jumped into the water. Everyone thought I was nuts! Rocks were pelting my body in the rough surf. All I felt were the waves rushing over me. It was a wonderful feeling, and I knew this was where I wanted to be, and the Pacific Coast of California was my home.

Pop didn't connect with the job he wanted, so our family drove to Seattle, Washington, where he had another brother. We stayed in my Uncle Joe's house with him, his wife, Nellie; sons, Leland and Ronnie; and daughter, JoNell, for about a month. I got a clerical job in downtown Seattle. During this time, I developed a kissing-cousin relationship with Ronnie. He and I went roller skating almost every evening. We danced the waltz on skates and could skate backward with precision. Needless to say, this kinship was improper. It worried my parents and aunt and uncle. Luckily, my dad got a call from a bus company in Inglewood, California, that wanted him. I quit my job, kissed my cousin good-bye, and Mom, Pop, my brother, and I headed back to California in our reliable little Studebaker car.

My parents rented an apartment in Inglewood. I started to work for the International Association of Machinists (IAM) Union, near LAX Airport, where all the airplane manufacturing plants in the Los Angeles area were located. Labor unions were heavily ensconced in the commercial and military aircraft industry. Their power in all-union shops was immense. If an employee did not pay his initiation fee or union dues within a specified time frame, he was fired from the aircraft company. Unions were at their apex in the aircraft manufacturing industry.

I saved my money. The job paid a handsome $1.30 an hour. This allowed me to give my parents seventy-five dollars a month for rent, and I had a few bucks left over to buy something nice for myself.

A 1952 Hawaiian bronze Studebaker convertible sat on the corner of a used car lot. It was the most beautiful car I had ever seen, with a sleek sports-car design, and looked just like new. I bought it. All I needed to do now was to learn how to drive. My dad delivered the car to me at work, and I was so excited that I ran out to greet him with a cigarette in my hand. It was an awkward moment when he looked down at my hand as I tried to hide the nasty smoke from his view. I had disappointed Pop. He patiently taught me to drive the car.

Moving from the corn belt to California was an opportunity and eye-opener. Instead of farms and railroads, there were bountiful business opportunities, a temperate climate, the vast Pacific Ocean, and towering mountains and verdant valleys. The people I met were fun-loving and outgoing—opposite the introverted and sheltered people I had grown up with.

Catalina Party Time

A couple of girls at work became my friends. They introduced me to some boys who lived in the coastal community of San Pedro, a small town with hilltop houses overlooking Los Angeles Harbor. Most of the men in San Pedro were Italian and Greek fishermen, with large families. Their sons were all cute. These boys were different than Iowa boys—more aggressive and strong-willed. I had to cross my legs to keep from being pestered by testosterone-laden guys trying to hit on me.

On a warm and sunny weekend, my girlfriends and I decided to take a steamship out of Los Angeles Harbor to Catalina Island, about twenty miles off the coastline. None of us had been to Catalina before. The ship held over a hundred passengers; most were frolic-in-the- sun partygoers.

Our little group of young ladies was noticed by a pack of guys sitting on the ship's railing. They invited us to the back of the boat to have a little libation with them. We thought that sounded cool, and off we went to an experience we were not prepared to handle.

When the ship anchored at the wharf in Catalina Harbor, the boys offered to carry our luggage to the hotel. We thought this was a generous offer and accepted. After checking into our room, my girlfriends and I went into the bathroom to comb our hair. When we had freshened up, a big surprise awaited us when we opened the bathroom door. These blankety-blank guys had taken off with our suitcases and purses. They were nowhere to be found.

We had no choice except to be on an extreme diet for the next three days. Of all things, I started my period and had no money to buy provisions to accommodate this untimely occurrence. My girlfriends and I ate a popsicle for dinner.

I was expecting my boyfriend, Joe, from San Pedro to come over to Catalina. We had been dating, and I had dinner at his parents' house with him the week before. He arrived the next day. After telling him my sad story, he bought me lunch and invited me to the beautiful and famous Catalina Ball Room to dance that evening (what a magical night). After the orchestra quit playing, he walked me back to the hotel where I was staying.

Bad news again—a bunch of rabble-rousing boys were having a party with the girlfriends I was sharing the room with. The hotel authorities kicked everyone out, so none of us had anywhere to sleep. My friend Joe said he could sneak me into the place where he and his buddies were staying. The magical evening was turning into a nightmare.

We walked down the hill to his digs and climbed over a tall chain-link fence into the compound where his little hut was located. His buddies were drunk. I gathered a bunch of chairs around me and, in a stern tone, told them to leave me alone. My bed was the bare floor, no pillow or blankets. I tucked myself in tightly between the chairs.

Early the next morning, I woke to guys snoring, the stink of vodka, and trash everywhere. I unwound myself from the chairs and sneaked out of the hut, over the fence, and back to the hotel where everything had gone haywire. I talked the hotel clerks into letting me back into our room so I could clean up.

My girlfriends and I returned to the mainland the next day, and when I went home, I was too embarrassed to tell my parents about my misadventure. My relationship with Joe cooled mightily.

A friend who worked with me lived in Lomita with her parents and two brothers. One of those brothers, Bill Boyes, was engaged to be married.

My girlfriends and I were hanging out at the popular Hot-In-Tot drive-in restaurant on Pacific Coast Highway, on a wintry Friday evening. This guy Bill was there too. After socializing and eating hamburgers, we decided, just for the heck of it, to drive up to Big Bear in the San Bernardino Mountains. Bill and I ended up in the same car. I had never been to the local mountains before and oohed and aahed all the way up the steep mountain road. It had become quite cold, and there was a lot of snow. The drive was fun, but it took hours to reach the highway summit. One of the boys had some scotch, which I had never tasted before, but to this day, if I am in the snow, scotch sounds good.

We played in the snow all day, going up and down the hills on rented sleds. On the way home Bill proposed to me and said he was going to get de-engaged from the other girl, who happened to be a minister's daughter. Bill's mom and stepdad belonged to the holy-roller church where the father of this girl was pastor.

Bill followed through on his disengagement to the minister's daughter and bought me an engagement ring.

The era of the 1950s is equated to an age of innocence in America. Life was uncluttered with uncertainty. We lived within our means and took commitments seriously. Trust was given in an unspoken handshake. There were no traffic jams or gangs in Los Angeles. Female high school students didn't get pregnant, and no one that I socialized with knew anything about drugs. Christmas and birthday presents were essential items, not frivolous toys or gadgets.

I looked forward to marriage and becoming a mother because my parents' marriage was a long-lasting, loving relationship. I hoped that I could find a man as good as my dad and that I could be as good a mom as my mom.

CHAPTER 3

Marriage; Parenthood; Space Age

Husband—Bill Boyes

The early 1950s was a great time for Mom and Pop to buy one of the thousands of well-constructed, inexpensive houses being built in Los Angeles and the surrounding area, but they passed up that opportunity.

Pop worked as a diesel mechanic at a bus company. Both my parents were entering the time in their lives when their children moved on to make their own lives. I brought Bill over to meet them. My mom asked Bill if he liked to fish (her standard for a down-to-earth person). Luckily, he answered her in the affirmative. Bill and I started making wedding plans.

The two of us had a traditional wedding at the First Baptist Church in Inglewood on April 17, 1954. My cousin, Sue, loaned me her long white wedding gown. Pop proudly marched me down the aisle, my mom cried, and my brother was there in his air force uniform. When pictures came back from the photo studio, I noticed that my shoes were on the wrong feet. I held to my goal of being a virgin on my wedding night.

Bill was working for Douglas Aircraft Company in El Segundo as an aircraft mechanic, making enough money so that I could quit work.

We decided to make the plunge of buying a home. A new tract of houses, located in the hills of Palos Verdes Peninsula, was within our financial reach. The house cost $12,500, and our payments, including taxes and insurance, were seventy-eight dollars a month. It had a big back yard, two bedrooms, and one bath.

Babies were on the agenda. After a few months went by, I was pregnant My tummy popped right out in front of me. I started wearing smocks at three months and grew fast. By the time I was eight months pregnant, I couldn't get my hands around my big stomach.

On Bill's and my first anniversary I was nine months pregnant and huge. A candlelight dinner in our dining room was all we could muster.

Sons—Bob and Rex

Our son Bob was born May 30, 1955, by caesarean section, weighing nine pounds, seven ounces. He was one month late. The doctor said I was not capable of giving birth to a baby this large. X-rays had shown my small pelvic area and our baby's large body and head.

My mom came to stay with us just prior to when the baby was due. By the time he was finally born, she had gone back home, and I was on my own.

No one had to ask whose child was ours in the hospital nursery. Our baby looked just like Bill. He was husky, had no chin, a big chest, and was as bald as a cue ball, just like his dad. We named him William Robert Boyes, and decided to call him Bob, so as not to confuse him with his dad, or get the nickname Billy-Bob.[5]

---

5   Ironically, when Bob became a sailboat racer, his mates called him Billy-Bob.

Bob sat up at three months and walked at nine months. He was strong, learned fast, and had a mind of his own! I tried to raise him according to Dr. Spock, the baby guru book author of that era. Dr. Spock said a baby should eat at regular hours and needed all his nutrients. I almost force-fed the poor kid, ringing a bell above his head so he opened his mouth, allowing me to spoon the spinach past his lips. I had regimented baby raising standards. However, I loved being a mom. I nursed Bob until he was three months old, and then stopped because he had six teeth.

While our son went through the terrible twos, I had been having severe pain in my feet. Surgery was required to correct the problem. Large bunions were cut off on all four sides of my feet. Tending a rambunctious little boy while I was unable to put any pressure on my feet was a challenge. I scooted around the house on a wheeled chair, propelling myself backwards with my heels.

No sooner had I recovered from this surgery, when another problem popped up. I developed grapefruit-size cysts on my ovaries. The doctors performed an exploratory on me to remove the cysts but left enough of my ovaries to get pregnant. I had a miscarriage about a year later (we went on a picnic, and I was clowning around and stood on my head. Don't know if this caused it, but that night I started bleeding).

We lived in a neighborhood where other young couples were in the same child-rearing era as us. Special occasion parties and dances were held in either our home or in the home of one of our neighbors. No one had extra money to spend on entertainment or restaurants. Bill and I went through the transition of drinking soda pop to having a beer once in a while.

We were both good jitterbuggers. Bill got overzealous with whipping me around at one party, and he threw me over his shoulder. I landed on my head. Several vertebrae were injured and sore. It took a few days to heal.

Two of Bill's longtime friends and their wives were our best friends. We spent weekends at the junkyard scavenging boat and engine parts. We found a worn-out and dilapidated fourteen foot boat and an old bedroom headboard (which turned into a dashboard for our boat). A rudimentary ski boat took shape. The hull was made of heavy wood, with little attention paid to fine craftsmanship. The guys painted the boat white with blue trim. When an old 50-horsepower Mercury engine was found in the junkyard and mounted on the stern, we were ready to launch our yacht. This was our first attempt at boat building.

Yearly vacations at a little resort on Lake Havasu called Black Meadows Landing were what we lived for. Warm, crystal blue water beckoned fun-seeking boaters. The land surrounding Lake Havasu is bone-dry. Scorpions, rattlesnakes, thorny trees, scorching sand, and hot wind kept anyone from venturing too far from the lake.

All three couples saved soda pop bottle five-cent refunds to finance our yearly trips. We packed our boat with food, cooking supplies, sleeping bags, bathing suits, and scruffy shoes.

The boat we never got around to naming wasn't fast enough to pull me up on a water ski, but it had room for six adults and our little boy. Whenever we pulled alongside a ski boat, I threw them a beer and asked if they would take me skiing. This always worked.

We picnicked under a big mesquite tree next to the beach on a particularly hot afternoon. A boat came into our anchorage, and the guys aboard were taking shore starts on their ski run. I wanted to try this.

All the guys were two-hundred-pound muscle-packed skiers. With one foot on the sand and one foot placed in their ski binding (which was balanced on top of the water) the skier took several feet of slack ski line looped in his hands and told the boat driver to hit it. The boat took off at full speed, while the skier popped right on top of the water and went off on a ski ride.

After drinking a beer with them, they asked if I wanted to try a shore start. I figured I had the trick wired. I stood on the shoreline, one foot in the ski, the other in the shallow water. I took several loops of slack in the ski line. I told the boat driver to hit it. This propelled me several feet into the air, before landing in the water face-first. A couple more tries, with less slack, were still not working. Finally, I figured out that I was a lightweight that didn't need any slack in the line. When the ski line was taut, I yelled, "Hit it!" Off I went, skiing like a pro!

When I came back to shore, I heard our little boy crying. I had put Bob on top of a picnic table for a nap. He was covered with ants. I guess everyone was in the water and didn't hear him crying. I ran down to the water with him in my arms and dunked the both of us into the lake, feeling guilty about not being an attentive mother but sure happy to have taken a shore start.

The campground at Black Meadows Landing was sizzling, about 115 degrees. The guys put up a twenty-by-twenty-foot cook tent, then rigged a sprinkler on top. The hot wind blowing through the mesh windows met with the water cascading down the outside of the tent, creating a cool breeze. This gave us air conditioning while we were preparing meals or eating.

Everyone slept on cots under the stars. In the middle of the day we paid the Black Meadows Landing store owner twenty-five cents for a block of ice. He also let us walk through his icehouse. The first year we vacationed at Lake Havasu we took four cases of soda pop and one case of beer. The following years, we took one case of soda pop and four cases of beer.

Liberation for women began in 1960, with the introduction of oral contraceptives! This marvelous little pill gave women control over their lives.

The following dubious birth control method could now be abolished: run into the bathroom after sex, shove a rubber shower hose up your whatsit and let the faucet (where the loose hose was somewhat attached) run wide open for a goodly amount of time. The hose invariably fell off the faucet, getting the whole bathroom drenched, unless the hose was held tightly on the faucet with the arm that wasn't busy. Most women had this setup in their bathtub to perform the defensive tactic of not getting pregnant. It worked pretty well.

Bill received an offer to go to work for Hughes Research Laboratories in Newport Beach, as an assistant metallurgist. This was a great advancement for him. We sold our Palos Verdes house and moved south to a little town called Costa Mesa. We bought a house in a recently developed subdivision. I was pregnant.

Bob was six years old when our son Rex was born on April 19, 1961. Rex was a beautiful baby, smaller than Bob, because he was taken by cesarean section two weeks early. We were a happy family, raising two sons in a brand-new house in Costa Mesa that had three bedrooms and two bathrooms, plus a big front and back yard.

America was coming of age. In 1955, the Salk vaccine became available, ending the plague of polio. Bob was inoculated against this debilitating disease when he was five years old. We lined up with him at school with other parents, while the kids got their priceless shots. Thankfully, no one in our extensive family was afflicted with this crippling disease.

The first credit card was introduced in 1958. We didn't get one until years later. The process was foreign to us. A family budget was a serious and on-going endeavor, closely monitored and adhered to.

Space Age and Cuba Embargo

In a surprise move, the Soviets launched the world's first satellite, Sputnik, in 1957, inaugurating the space age. In 1961 they launched a vehicle that carried the first man, Yuri Gargarin, into space. They had beaten us into orbit above the planet Earth; however, we were not far behind.

Later that year, the United States launched its first man into space, Alan Shepherd. My dad was enamored with space technology. The space age was beyond our wildest imagination.

John F. Kennedy was elected president in 1960. He brought our nation together. Kennedy announced that our country could put a man on the moon within that decade. The space program geared up to meet the challenge. We Americans were supportive of the mission, and thousands of our youth signed up for engineering and science courses in college.

Fidel Castro came to power in a rebellion against the Cuban premier, Zaldivar, in 1959. He seized American-owned properties in Cuba, oil refineries, sugar mills, and electric utilities.

The infamous Bay of Pigs invasion was an unsuccessful attempt by US-backed Cuban exiles to overthrow the government of Cuban dictator Fidel Castro. On April 17, 1961, two days before my son Rex was born, CIA-trained Cuban exiles landed at Cochinos (Bay of Pigs). The local Cuban population did not support the exiles. Newly elected President Kennedy decided against using American air power in support of the exiles. Castro's army won. The Kennedy administration was seriously embarrassed by the failure of the invasion.

Relations between Soviet Secretary General Nikita Khrushchev and Cuban Secretary General Fidel Castro were excellent because Cuba had no military defense against the United States, and strategically, Cuba was a valuable place for the Soviets, just ninety miles off the Florida coast. Khrushchev tried to set up nuclear weapons on the small island.

America stood on the brink of nuclear war. We were scared as hell. Our cars were loaded with flashlights, blankets, first-aid kits, and non-perishable food and water. Friends and neighbors built underground bomb shelters. The catchphrase better-dead-than-red was born.

We had a little boy and a baby to protect. Bill and I joined the ultraright-wing John Birch Society. Every week we attended political meetings. A radicalized John Bircher scared the be-jesus out of us at those meetings by apoplectically implying that Russia might nuke us, unless we nuked them first.

The Cuban Missile Crisis existed for two weeks in October 1962. Soviet missiles in Cuba, disguised as trees, were aimed at various cities in the United States. Kennedy called for a blockade of Cuba on October 24, 1962. The blockade worked--the Soviet ships reversed course. Kennedy was able to talk Khrushchev into disabling the missiles on October 26.

Kennedy had backed Nikita Khrushchev into a corner by standing his ground. The Soviets knew if the missiles were not removed, America would attack the Soviet Union. Our capabilities were superior to that of our threatening enemy.

The Soviets erected the Berlin Wall to stop the mass exodus of people fleeing Soviet East Berlin for West Berlin and the non-Communist world in 1961. The wall was a mass of concrete, barbed wire, and stone that cut into the heart of the city, separating families and friends. For twenty-eight years it stood as a grim symbol of the gulf between the Communist East and the democratic West.

On January 20, 1963, President Kennedy delivered a speech that electrified an adoring crowd gathered in the shadow of the Berlin Wall. As he paid tribute to the spirit of Berliners and to their quest for freedom, the crowd roared with approval upon hearing the president's dramatic pronouncement: "Ich bin ein Berliner" (I am a Berliner).

On June 11, 1963, President Kennedy proposed a strong civil rights bill to Congress, but southern Democrats in Congress managed to block the bill in committee.

Assassination of a President

John F. Kennedy was fatally wounded by gunshots while riding in a presidential motorcade through Dallas, Texas on November 22, 1963.

The news of Kennedy's death shocked everyone. In cities around the world, people wept openly. Motor traffic came to a halt as news of Kennedy's death spread from car to car. All three news networks canceled programming for the next three days to provide nonstop coverage of the assassination. It was the largest TV news event in history.

When the announcement came over the TV network that President Kennedy had been assassinated, I was sitting in the living room watching television with my baby, Rex, in my arms. Hearing my call, Bill and Bob came into the house from working in the yard to watch the surreal scene unfold on TV. I cried and thought the world is experiencing a terrible tragedy and loss. This fair minded, intelligent, and revered president had been silenced.

Our family grieved the loss of President Kennedy and watched his widow, Jackie, hold the Bible for the presidential swearing-in ceremony of Vice President Lyndon Johnson aboard Air Force One while flying back to Washington. She stood stoically, still wearing blood-soaked clothes from the gunshot wounds that killed her husband. The Camelot family, whom we admired, had been torn apart. Our popular president had been replaced with Lyndon Johnson, a forlorn giant of a man, who I had a difficult time liking.

Representatives from over ninety countries attended the funeral, including the Soviet Union. After the service, the casket containing Kennedy's body was taken by caisson to Arlington Cemetery for burial. The modest-looking eternal flame burns at the site.

Lyndon Johnson acceded to the presidency in 1963 and won reelection in 1964 when he ran against Republican conservative Barry Goldwater. Bill and I voted for Goldwater because he was not going to allow Vietnam to bring our nation to its knees.

Vietnam War

We were a nation that needed to heal and not go to war. In what was to be the downfall of his presidency, Johnson began an escalation of American commitment in the Vietnam conflict.

American aircraft attacked North Vietnamese gunboats on August 5, 1964, in what became known as the Tonkin Gulf Incident. This profligate action was the prelude to our long and bloody battle in the jungles of Vietnam.

A former Vietnam War US Marine general and Medal of Honor recipient, Smedley Butler, said in a speech on May 14, 1966:

"You read, you're televised to, you are preached to that it is necessary that we have our armed forces fight, get killed and maimed, and kill and maim other human beings including women and children because now is the time we must stop some kind of unwanted ideology from creeping up on this nation."

The Vietnam War Pentagon Papers revealed that our government had deliberately expanded its role in the war by conducting air strikes over Laos and raids on the coast of North Vietnam, while President Johnson had been promising not to expand the war.

Eventually, there were just not enough volunteers to fight a protracted war. The government reinstituted the draft.

Thank God my two sons were too young to be drafted. As the deaths mounted, the Johnson administration was met with the full weight of American antiwar sentiment. Protests erupted on college campuses and spread across the country.

In another horrific stain on our national dignity, presidential candidate Robert F. Kennedy was assassinated after addressing supporters at the Ambassador Hotel in Los Angeles on June 5, 1968. He was much like his brother, in that his best and most fruitful years could never be realized, unknown to history. Robert Kennedy was unabashedly sympathetic to the plight of the poor.

President Johnson was not a likable man. After numerous

accomplishments in civil rights, the Vietnam War brought him down, and it is the war that Americans equate him with. It suffocated Johnson.

Bill and I were disgusted with American foreign policy. Watching the news brought tears to our eyes. Our family was the most important aspect of our lives and what we cherished most.

Raising a Family

Bob was in school and was a delightful child. Rex was a handful. He got into everything and was not the good kid Bob was. Bob kept his room clean and was helpful with household chores. Rex's room was a mess, and he didn't care. He was mischievous. Nothing from Dr. Spock's book on raising children seemed to work. Rex could charm the socks off of strangers, but I was wise to his shenanigans.

Being a stay-at-home-mom suited me at this stage of my life. The kids brought completeness to Bill's and my marriage. We were still living payday to payday, but a semblance of order was at hand. Bill was doing well at Hughes Research. For a guy who had no formal education, he was working in a professional atmosphere and was surrounded by degreed metallurgists doing nascent innovative work on gallium arsenide computer chips.

Our social life was full. Neighbors and friends we met through Bill's work came to our house for dinner, or we went to parties and dinners at their homes.

My parents were an integral part of our lives. Mom and Pop

|*My sons, Bob and Rex, and me*|

came to our home frequently for the weekend, and always on holidays. We were a close family.

Newport Beach Back Bay was a few miles away from our house. It offered a quiet place to launch our ski boat. I loved water skiing out into the ocean, beyond the wave line between Newport Beach and Oceanside. Big rollers carried the boat and me high in the air, or down into a trough, creating a perfect water skiing experience. This is before surfboards and kayaks. The coastal ocean was free of most other human activity.

Bob and his dad were members of the youth-group Indian Guides. Bill's Indian name was Bald Eagle because of the lack of hair on his noggin. Bob's name was Little Eagle. They enjoyed their powwow getaways in the San Gabriel Mountains.

With an eye on future employment in office management, I started to take business classes at the local junior college in Costa Mesa. The next-door neighbor and I traded babysitting chores while we both took classes.

For a lark, I joined the intermural college swim team, where I improved my stroke and swim speed. This was an important and valuable decision; however, I did not realize it at the time. Involvement in triathlons was decades away, where the importance of a powerful swim stroke was vital to the mastery of the triathlon.

A couple of books I read about this time of my life, entitled *Atlas Shrugged* and *The Fountainhead*, by Ayn Rand, sparked an inner light. It spoke to my beliefs of personal responsibility and attacking a problem with gusto. Rand was an ultraconservative author who wrote many novels and political treatise espousing her take-no-prisoners philosophy. I thought she spoke to a perfect world, without greed, where it was possible to accomplish goals, with no thought for those who were not strong and resolute. Where I thought her genius came through was her belief of bringing the best out in people who followed moralistic principles. I have always had a pragmatic approach to difficulties and problems. Rand reinforced my attitude and challenged my mind to the point where intellectual growth became important to me—at last!

During the 1960s, my dad sat with Bob, drawing planets, moons, and rocketships on weekend get-togethers. There was a surreal aspect to America's space program, but everyone was excited about Kennedy's aspiration of going to the moon within a decade. We were proud of our country.

The Apollo 11 mission was launched from Cape Kennedy, Florida, on July 16, 1969. Our family was glued to the TV. All of America was spellbound. The moon landing, arguably the most astonishing technological achievement in history, took place on July 20, 1969.

During the lunar landing, NASA astronaut Neil Armstrong took manual control of the lunar module *Eagle* and piloted it away from a rocky area to a safe landing. His first words from the moon were: "Houston, Tranquility Base here. The *Eagle* has landed."

Several hours later, he climbed out of the lunar module and became the first person to walk on the moon and said:

"That's one small step for man, one giant leap for mankind."

There is a small lunar crater named in his honor near the Apollo 11 landing site.

America had surpassed the Soviet Union's space program. We left them in the moon dust!

Bill decided to quit his metallurgy job at Hughes Research and go into sales at a microscope company. This was not an economically wise decision. Bill's ability to sell was impaired by his lack of college education and business background. He worked hard and was a good husband, but our income suffered because of the job change.

We sold our home in Costa Mesa to my brother and his family and moved to Thousand Oaks in the late 1960s. This was a great place to raise kids. Bob was ten, and Rex was four. The house we bought sat on a double cul-de-sac. We could play ball, skateboard, and have barbecues in the middle of the street. Our neighbors were social, and we had lots of parties.

Rex was a bright kid. We enrolled him into St. Patrick's Episcopal Grammar School. He was capable of reading the *Wall Street Journal* in first grade. Obviously, he didn't understand what he was reading, but he could read and pronounce the words correctly. Both boys were growing up as strong individuals.

Our neighbors across the street went water skiing every summer at Bass Lake, just outside of Yosemite National Park. As our friendship grew, they invited us to join them. We loved the place. The lake is surrounded by pine trees, with crystal-clear blue water, beckoning us to launch the boat and open her up to take a ski run. The falls area at the head of the lake provided us hours of sliding down humungous granite stones, from one waterfall to the next. We wore out a lot of bathing suits in our pursuit to see who could slide the farthest. The kids and I held ski-offs on the lake in the evening, making deep cuts and jumping across the wake. We skied our hearts out. Bill drove the boat. Our family laughed and ribbed each other unmercifully.

This was the presunscreen era; the harsh and damaging effects of sunray exposure were not well known. I lathered up with Crisco lard. I not only smelled like fried chicken, I was the same color as fried chicken. When ridding in the boat, I slipped from one side to the other, and when I fell while water skiing, I scooted across the water like a slick Frisbee.

Bob and Rex were close. but there was brotherly rivalry between them. They were talented athletes—their physiques strong and slim. Any extreme sport attracted them.

Rex could belch a whole paragraph and keep us in stitches with jokes he told. He laughed as hard as we did. Bob was the strong, quiet one. The two boys wrestled and called each other names, but came together and played on the same team. I enjoyed being their mom.

When Bob started high school, he signed up for the swim team. He had grown into a handsome teenager and had a girlfriend.

One of Bob's hobbies was motocross motorcycle racing. Bill and I didn't like the long-haired kids involved in the sport. We told Bob that if he sold his bike and gave up motocross, a sailboat might be in our future. He sold his bike the next day.

I told the kids that buying a sailboat meant I needed to get a job. They had to take over more of the household maintenance chores. Both boys told me that they could paint, mow the lawn, and clean the house better than I, so no problem!

The first place I applied for a job I was hired. A CPA/attorney in Thousand Oaks brought me onboard as an office manager.

New Adventure—Sailing

Bob was fourteen and Rex was eight when we bought our first sailboat—a twenty-four-foot Cal named *Capriccio*. This small sailboat had three foot of headroom down below deck. We moored her in a slip in Channel Islands Harbor.

The kids picked up sailing like sponges. The endeavor changed our lives. Friday afternoons, we crowded into our little Volkswagen and headed for Channel Islands Harbor. We worked on the boat and sailed up and down the Ventura coastline, or out to Anacapa Island, thirteen miles out to sea.

Many of the boats on our dock sailed to the larger and more distant Santa Cruz Island for the weekend. As our expertise, or hubris, expanded, we took the leap and sailed to an anchorage on the island with them. The compass course was dead to weather, with gusty winds and big waves. We were learning on the fly, but managed to sail and anchor in every anchorage around the island. I cooked many meals on my knees in the galley of our tiny vessel. Nasty blows can come at any time. Sheltered coves meant a better chance of having a good night's sleep. That didn't always work. The wind could start howling out of any direction in the dead of night. We learned about good ground tackle, not leaving loose gear in the open cockpit, and tying up the dinghy securely before going to sleep in our bunks. The gentle lapping of waves against the hull and rocking motion of the boat put us into a deep slumber. If the halyards started slapping against the mast and the sound of wind came down into the cabin, we lay awake and hoped it stopped. Usually it didn't, so a two hour watch was set up with one person on-deck as a lookout for an anchor breaking loose, setting us adrift. All four of us learned quickly that we were at the mercy of Mother Nature.

Bob was intrigued with boats flying their voluminous spinnakers in offshore sailboat races. He quickly became immersed in the sport with local sailors. He crewed on their boats and showed a natural ability to race a sailboat.

Bill and I decided to buy a twenty-nine-foot Islander named *Valero* and get the entire family into racing. It was a giant step up from our first boat. The Islander had six foot of head-room, a large galley area, and a head! The boat was somewhat competitive.

As Bob started to win more races, Rex was following in his footsteps, so we made the plunge to buy a higher-tech boat, a twenty-nine-foot Ranger. This boat had a taller mast, a fin keel, and was lighter weight. We named the boat *Saltshaker*. (A popcorn-eating boat-naming session in our living room ended when one of us asked Bob to pass the saltshaker.)

Santa Cruz Island is a natural wonderland for sailors, scuba divers, kayakers, and hikers. It lies twenty-six miles northwest of the Ventura County coastline. The island is large, approximately twenty-five miles long and four miles wide. Water caves embedded in the rocky cliffs are accessible by dinghy and kayak. Exploring these dark, drippy caverns is exciting. Giant seals and fish swim underwater inside the caves, surging in and out with the wave action. The bottom of the sea can be clearly seen. Bright yellow flowers are growing on the sea floor near the caves. The flowers turn dark at cave entrances.

After anchoring the boat in an island cove and settling into our home on the water, we piled in the rubber dinghy and rode through water caves. At high tide our heads crunched the roof of the cave when we picked up speed on top of a wave. The ocean swell propelled us out through another cave entrance. We wanted to do it again—this was awesome!

Cliff diving was great fun. I did a giant swan dive off a pretty high cliff and landed wrong. My back felt like it was broken, but the next day we all jumped off the same cliff, except I did cannon balls instead of head-first dives. Hiking trails are all over the island, taking you to high vantage points where the sea is hundreds of feet below. The kids found Indian artifacts while digging around in the hills. Early Indian tribes hunted and fished around San Miguel, Santa Rosa, Santa Cruz, Anacapa, Santa Barbara, and Catalina islands.

Little Scorpion is a magnificent Santa Cruz Island anchorage. High cliffs ring the shoreline and an offshore rock protrusion houses a seagull rookery. On a weekend in the middle of summer several boats were anchored and enjoying the scenery. We noticed basking sharks swimming into the anchorage. One of the guys on the boat next to ours jumped in the water with his fins and mask to play around with the massive creatures, much to our delight. What a show.

Boats could most often count on strong northwest prevailing wind and ocean swell in the late afternoon. A perfect spot to anchor was close to the cliffs and sheltered from wind and swell. If too many boats tried to anchor in one area, invariably, someone's anchor crossed another boat's anchor, causing that boat to be set adrift. This never happened in calm water, but late in the day when the wind was strongest. Boats came into the anchorage after sailing across the channel waters from the mainland. Everyone was exhausted, wet and cold, anxious to get their sails down and stowed, and anchors set. This was a setup for all hell breaking loose. Boats came within a hair's breadth of crashing into one another.

My favorite scene to watch, if we were safely anchored in our own little spot, played out again and again. Usually the wife stood on the bow, ready to throw the anchor overboard as soon as her husband, who was on the tiller, called out to her. The boat approached the anchoring spot. Between tangles in the anchor line, the boat moving too fast, and no one hearing what the other person was saying, the *f* word was shouted at the wife, while she shouted it right back to her husband. We were in a knee-slappin' howl. Eventually, the boat was anchored.

On a late summer weekend our family sailed out of Channel Islands Harbor and headed out to Scorpion Anchorage, on the southeast shore of Santa Cruz Island. We had light wind and smooth sailing across the channel, sailing into anchorage by midafternoon. Saturday evening was pleasant. Rex was playing cards on a boat off our stern with a bunch of other kids. Bob, his girlfriend, Bill, and I were relaxing on the stern of *Saltshaker* just after dinner. The wind suddenly died, and it became warm and still. Without warning, the wind and seas picked up out of the east, the opposite of a prevailing wind and sea. We were about to get hit with a destructive Santa Ana wind. Everything on deck started flying. The boat started to heave as steep waves came into the anchorage.

There was no way to reach Rex and get him back onboard our boat. His boat had a flopper stopper in the water, which had to be hauled in and tied down (difficult in a gale). A sail cover was on the main. It had to be removed and the mainsail needed to be hoisted, because the outboard motor on the back of the boat didn't work. Rex, the youngest but most experienced sailor on board, had the other three kids get life jackets on. He was thirteen years old. The owner of the boat was on another boat, which had been anchored close to shore. Several boats were on the verge of getting washed up on the rocky cliffs behind them.

Everyone in the anchorage cut their anchor lines, trying desperately to make headway out of the anchorage. Our inboard engine was running at full speed. We could see that Rex had the mainsail up on his boat. It was a sobering moment. Our boat was headed out to sea and our son Rex was in a hell of a mess. There were deep black holes in the ocean, created by waves building from the east. Our boat plowed into them. The small twenty-three-foot boat Rex was on had no radio. We started calling the coast guard from *Saltshaker*'s radio to alert them of boats that were stranded helplessly in the anchorage. We were more than twenty-six miles off the coastline. It took well into the night to reach Channel Islands Harbor. We were assured that the coast guard was doing everything it could to rescue endangered boats. Bill and Bob stayed on *Saltshaker* the rest of the night, in case they got a call on the marine radio. I went home to be near the telephone.

About eight o'clock the next morning, Rex phoned me at home. I asked him where he was blown to, Hawaii, or Santa Barbara. He told me that it took three hours of tacking back and forth across the anchorage to finally get clear of the rocky cliffs. The wind was blowing directly at them. There was no way he could head east toward Channel Islands Harbor, so he peeled the boat off northwest. He said that by morning the wind let up and he coasted into Santa Barbara Harbor. *Whew!* We were so relieved he and the other kids were safe. All he needed to do now was to sail the boat forty-eight miles down the coast to Channel Islands Harbor.

The next weekend we had a big dock party to celebrate our sea adventure and laugh and shout about how a freak wind had caused such life-threatening havoc.

We joined Anacapa Yacht Club in Channel Islands Harbor, where the kids, Bill, and I were plunged into a new social order. One must be a member of a yacht club to race. We were brought from novice sailing into sailboat racing with the big boys. They became our friends, competitors, and mates. It became apparent there was a pecking order between experienced and inexperienced sailors. We had to learn the lingo, drink Coors beer, not make a fool of ourselves on the race course, and be thick-skinned. It helped to be cool.

My Father Dies

Our family boat outings did not include my parents, who were not ocean savvy. They came to our home for Thanksgiving and Christmas, but we each had our own lives. When my father was sixty-four years old, his health failed. He had a lump on his head. Mom talked him into going to the doctor, who informed them both to "get your house in order." Pop had cancer, and half his skull was eaten away.

He lasted six months. The cancer started in his lungs and traveled through his bloodstream. Pop had surgery to remove the tumor on his brain. It looked like he might recover for a short time, but his body was riddled with the last stages of cancer. During the last month of his life, his mind stopped working, yet doctors wanted to operate on his hip, which was disintegrating. I asked a medical team to stop moving this man, who was groaning during a hospital examination. The dignity of dying is diminished by last-ditch efforts to prolong the inevitable. Tremendous amounts of money are spent lengthening the road to death.

Our family visited Pop at the hospital every weekend. He died a few weeks shy of his sixty-fifth birthday, the date he and Mom had planned to begin their well-deserved retirement years fishing favorite streams and lakes and visiting Alaska.

Bill, the kids, and I were deeply overcome with grief. Pop was my hero and the person I respected above all others. Bob and Rex had never experienced a death of anyone they knew before. Bill and I talked to them about keeping their grandmother in their prayers. We would miss the warm blanket of my father's love, his laughter, and his quiet strength.

Mom and Pop went everywhere together. Mom never learned to drive and was employed for just a couple of years of her life. She came to live with us in Thousand Oaks. She paid for a room and bath to be built onto the side of our house. We tried consoling her.

Bob was the one who could relate best with her. Part of Mom died when her cherished husband passed away.

Approximately one year later, Mom went to a dance and bingo game for seniors. When the band began playing, a gentleman named Earl approached Mom and asked her to dance. That was the beginning of a fast relationship. She and Earl married a few months after they met. Mom moved to Earl's house in Long Beach. We were happy Mom had met someone to fill the vacuum in her life. No one could replace Pop. Mom's capacity for moving on carried her into a new life.

Ponzi Scheme

The guy I worked for in Thousand Oaks was in hot water. His father met me at his son's business office and said his son had suffered a massive heart attack and could not communicate with anyone, except his dad. My sympathy went out to the family. Strangely, no one could get the name of the hospital—we wanted to send flowers and let the guy know we hoped he recovered quickly.

This was my first job in seventeen years. He had given me responsibility, guidance in learning business bookkeeping, and gave my rusty shorthand abilities a workout through numerous technical letters and documents. I thought highly of his expertise.

After several weeks of misinformation, the truth came out. My CPA/attorney boss had been arrested for selling nonexistent airplanes to the US government.

This guy was an experienced and well-respected professional, in the run for a city council seat, a Boy Scout leader, and was in a business venture with the mayor of Thousand Oaks, buying post offices and medical buildings for tax shelters.

The local professional community signed on the dotted line for the limited partnership tax shelters.

Various mortgage payments on the tax shelter buildings became due. The mayor and I pieced together the limited partnership's financial analysis, gathered the participants in his office, and explained that my nefarious boss had fraudulently used the limited partnership's deposits from investors to buy more medical buildings and post offices, without fully subscribing the ones he had already purchased.

Consequently, the partnership participants (mostly medical doctors) lost their money and got a 100 percent tax write-off the first year of their investment. The money was gone—lost in perpetuity. The fraudulent investment scheme created havoc in the affluent Thousand Oaks community. Everyone was incredulous that a highly respected community leader and upstanding family man was a crook.

I had seen signs that all was not well. On a late afternoon, just before his disappearance, I walked from my office back to my boss's office. He was sitting at his desk sweating heavily, one hand tightly gripping his chair, the other holding the telephone receiver. The look on his face was ghastly. I quickly closed his door to give him privacy. When he came out of his office, he acted as though nothing had happened.

The FBI closed the office and confiscated all of the records. My boss served time in prison and lost both his law and CPA license. I lost my job.

CHAPTER 4

Midlife Changes; Tragedy; Sailing

School, Work, Sailing

In the late 1960s, we sold our Thousand Oaks home and moved to Oxnard to be near our sailboat. Rex went to a Seventh-day Adventist school in El Rio. He had a hard time with Seventh-day Adventist religious philosophy but was a good student in his academic studies. On weekend school outings, Rex stuffed his clothes bag with beef jerky, which he sold to the vegetarian boys, who were not being supervised by food cops. Bill got a job at Hughes Research in Santa Barbara. I started to work for Petoseed Co., a horticultural firm in El Rio.

Bob graduated from high school and enrolled at Ventura Community College and, also, set up his own sailboat rigging business in the Channel Islands and Ventura harbor areas. He learned through the hard knocks of running a business that pleasing customers isn't always easy. They wanted him on their boat at a moment's notice, the job done yesterday, and at little cost.

Bill and I bought a small condo in Oxnard, about a mile away from the ocean. We usually managed to eat together in the evening, even though our schedules were hectic. In the midst of a dinner party with our friends, Bill and Rex were horsing around in the living room. Rex swallowed a fifty-cent piece. He was choking but then swallowed the large coin. Everyone got in the car and headed for the emergency room at the local hospital. The doctors x-rayed Rex's chest, and there was the fifty-cent piece. We were told it would dissolve in a few days, and Rex should watch for it. We all went home, much relieved and hungry. Bob had come home from a college class and found the table set and food in serving bowls. He figured something awful had happened, and he had better clean up the kitchen and put the food in the fridge. We all laughed while Rex explained to Bob that he expected the fifty-cent piece to turn to change: a quarter, a couple of dimes, and a nickel. Dinner was warmed up and devoured.

I quit smoking after reading an article in a magazine about "The Silent Ward" where people who had throat cancer had to have their larynx taken out, preventing them from ever speaking again. My throat was sore. This hit home. I reached into my purse, took the cigarettes out, and threw them in the trash. My sons hated my dirty habit. They put stink bombs and exploding tips in any cigarette packs I left lying around.

After work each day, instead of sitting down with Bill and having a glass of wine and a cigarette, I started running down to the marina where our boat was slipped. At first I thought I was going to die. Soon, my aerobic capacity improved. After a year of running and not smoking, I competed in a 10k footrace. When I crossed the finish line, my two sons picked me up in their arms, threw me in the air, and yelled, "Yeah, Mom!"

Our world was work, sailing, and school. Time was precious, and we tried to prioritize our schedules. Friday nights in Channel Islands Harbor aboard our boat was what our family looked forward to. The Whales Tail Restaurant was across the harbor from our dock. Our sailing friends and us rowed our dinghies to the Whales Tail dock, tied them up, and went into the restaurant bar. We listened to music played by a guy who strummed his guitar and sang just like Neil Diamond. Occasionally, the famous actor John Carradine sailed up to the dock, letting his sails nonchalantly drop to the deck. He'd then stomp up to the bar. Much to the delight of Bob and Rex, Carradine recited Shakespeare. His rapturous voice held us spellbound.

We talked about the Vietnam War with our kids and our hope that it would end soon. It was impossible to exterminate Communism in Asia. Vietnam was not a threat to America.

Ernest Hemingway wrote in *For Whom the Bell Tolls*: "War is mechanized doom using ugly toys."

Maleficent Actions in Government

Richard Nixon was elected president in 1968. His major goal was settlement of the Vietnam War. In his first inaugural address he talked about being a peacemaker. However, he came into office with a secret plan. It involved bringing troops home, while bombing Vietnam, Laos, and Cambodia to smithereens, rooting out Communist sanctuaries and supply routes.

The intense bombing campaigns taking place in the spring of 1970 sparked college campus protests across America. At Kent State University, in Ohio, four students were killed by National Guardsmen who were called out to preserve order on campus after days of anti-Nixon protests. Shock waves crossed the nation as students at Jackson State University in Mississippi were also shot and killed.

Attempting to defeat Communism in Asia, the Korean War, and then the Vietnam War interrupted our focus on building a peaceful society at home. Antiwar protesters clamored for the war to end. They held mass demonstrations in our capital and across the nation.

After Nixon unleashed a series of deadly bombings on North Vietnam's largest cities, the international community forced the Nixon administration to reconsider its tactics and strategy.

The killing was visceral. There was no reason to continue a war that wantonly destroyed villages of terrified citizens. Napalm bombs burned villagers to cinders.

When the *New York Times* began publishing the Pentagon papers in 1971, describing recommendations and decisions concerning our military actions under the Kennedy and Johnson administrations, President Nixon was incensed and protested that the papers should not be published. The case went to the Supreme Court, and in a six to three decision, the court said the government had not met the burden of proof, protecting an absolute right of free speech and the people's right-to-know. Cover-ups of war planning and execution should not be tolerated.

Our armed forces fought bravely to destroy the Viet Cong and North Vietnamese. Returning veterans were not given the respect they deserved from fellow Americans because of our country's immense condemnation for those that planned and carried out the Vietnam War. Our military fight and die for our country and are our most treasured asset.

Nixon was reelected in 1972 by a narrow margin. The president and his top aides were deeply involved in an extensive cover-up of the Democratic National Committee office break-in at the Watergate office complex in Washington, DC, and other White House-sanctioned illegal activities, such as the secret bombing of Cambodia in southeast Asia. Nixon ordered illegal wire taps of reporters and government employees to discover the source of news leaks about the bombing.

I heard G. Gordon Liddy, a conservative talk show host who was on Nixon's staff, boast about his participation in the break-in debacle on his radio show.

Nixon tried to shore up his presidency by opening a dialog with

China. His effort was sincere and caused diplomatic relations with China to be on a friendlier basis.

President Nixon resigned from office on August 4, 1974, because he was facing certain impeachment for his crimes in the Watergate scandal, becoming the only US president forced to resign.

Nixon left from the front lawn of the White House in the presidential helicopter, using his familiar arms spread above his head gesture, as if he was victoriously leaving to go on to other important presidential obligations.

When Gerald Ford came into office, he pardoned Nixon. This action sidestepped the fact the president was guilty. There was no moral judgment on the misconduct that had occurred in our government.

The Ford administration withdrew American troops from Vietnam. We had not stopped the spread of communism. This controversial war is still being hashed and rehashed.

An unlikely man, a peanut farmer, made it big. Jimmy Carter was elected president on the Democratic ticket in 1976.

In a very confrontational decision, Carter kept our athletes from participating in the 1980 Olympics in Moscow, because of Moscow's invasion of Afghanistan. I thought this boycott was terribly unfair to the athletes that had trained so hard and were not permitted to compete with their peers from around the world. Keep politics out of the Olympics!

The seizure of hostages at the US Embassy in Iran dominated the news during the last fourteen months of Carter's administration. There was a botched attempt to free the hostages in Tehran near the end of his presidency. Iran released the fifty-two Americans after Carter left office.

Everyone remembers President Carter wearing a sweater in the White House in order to conserve heating fuel. We drove our car to gasoline stations and waited in line to fill the gas tank. Gas was scarce due to the hostage crisis. Prices went through the roof, bringing inflation to the forefront of our economy. Interest rates climbed to 21 percent. Investing in long-term notes and bonds brought hefty returns. We didn't have any extra money, so could not take advantage of the investment opportunity.

In Carter's postpresidency he has been active in international peace negotiations and in bringing legitimate democratic elections into third world countries. In his Habitat for Humanity housing construction with his wife, Rosalyn, they help build dwellings for the world's indigent peoples. The Carter Center advances human rights and is committed to alleviating human suffering. He won the Nobel Peace Prize in 2002.

There is a lot of ill feeling toward Carter because of his support for a Palestinian state. I've always liked this ex-president because he works hard to help those in need.

Again, politics took a backseat in our lives, as sailing enveloped us.

Beach Home

Bill and I sold the condo in Oxnard and bought a condo on the Hollywood Beach peninsula, a narrow strip of land between the ocean and Channel Islands Harbor. The kids loved it. Surfboards were stacked in the garage, and sailboat racing was a big part of our agenda. Bob started to crew on bigger boats in races from California to Mexico and to Hawaii.

A sailboat race was on yacht club dockets every weekend.

|*Bob and Rex on Saltshaker*|

We raced them all. Like us, most of our sailing competitors kept their boats on B Dock, in front of the Lobster Trap Restaurant. We helped each other to get our boats ready for the next race.

The Ensenada Race was held in May. It is the world's largest international yacht race, with over six hundred entries. In order to get boats down south where the big race started, our local boats raced from Channel Islands Harbor to Newport Beach the week before.

In our first Ensenada Race, Bob skippered *Saltshaker*. Bill, Rex, and our friend Randy crewed. They took a surprising second place in the MORF (midget ocean racing fleet) sixty-boat division.

I cheered from the beach in Ensenada when I spotted our spinnaker in a telescope that was planted on the front lawn of our oceanfront cabin. *Saltshaker* was among much larger boats, whose spinnakers were propelling them toward the finish line. I knew they were doing well.

|*Saltshaker near the finish line of the Ensenada Race*|

The small group of yacht club friends who had been watching the race with me and I jumped in the car and headed for where the boats would finish. A long breakwater protects the harbor. I stopped the car and climbed over the guardrail so I could run out to the end of the breakwater to see *Saltshaker* cross the finish line. A Mexican police officer behind me yelled, "Alto!" I was unaware of what stop meant in Spanish, so I kept running. He had a gun pointed at my back. Luckily, my Mexican-savvy friends told the officer I was just a crazy gringo girl who was excited about the yacht race.

The next two days were wild. Anacapa Yacht Club rented a hotel suite with a balcony that overlooked a large courtyard. An elevated chalkboard stretched across the lawn of the courtyard, listed in what order the boats finished. This is where racers hung out to see if they won or lost. Margarita machines were everywhere, along with juiced-up sailors. We hung over the railing of AYC's hotel room verandah and watched the scene below, went down and partied with everyone, and then walked the streets of the town. This was a brand-new experience for our family. We were wild-eyed. Hussong's Bar was packed. I saw a girl lifted up over the heads of others in the jam-packed bar. She was passed overhead from guy to guy. When she was finally let down, she had no clothes on.

Bill and I started looking for Rex, who we had not seen for a couple of hours. Finally, we spotted him. He and our crew member, Randy, were wandering down the street, up to who knows what. Rex was gung-ho to do anything. Randy, a twenty-six-year-old wise guy and hellion, was the wrong person for our teenage son to be around. I took Rex by the ear and drove him back to our beach cabin.

The next day Bob, along with other sailors who did well, received their Ensenada trophies for the race from various American and Mexican dignitaries and military officers. Bands were blaring out the Mexican anthem. Rex and I cheered wildly as Bob held up his trophy for the world to see. We were standing on a cement donkey in the courtyard, and both fell to the ground in our exuberance.

It was time to motor-sail the boat back to San Diego to clear customs, and then sail north to Channel Islands Harbor.

Heavy yacht club involvement led me to become rear commodore for AYC. This meant that my race committee team and I ran seventy-two races a year. There were weekend races and Wet Wednesday races in the summer. I was responsible for setting the race course, hoisting the start flags, giving racers the horn as they crossed the finish line, computing the results, and getting those results into the Ventura newspapers and the *Los Angeles Times*. Instead of crewing on races, I spent my time watching *Saltshaker* race by while our race committee boat clocked her in, along with the other racers.

As the next year's Ensenada Race approached, I made time to crew aboard our boat. We won the pre-Ensenada Race between Channel Islands Harbor and Newport Harbor. Good omen. Boats are moored at the Newport Yacht Club until race day. Bob, Rex, and I drove to Newport Beach. When we got there, Bill and Randy were already on the boat. Randy had been nippin' the bottle and he was feeling no pain. There was last-minute work to get the boat ready for the big race the next day. I decided to take Randy over to my brother's house in nearby Costa Mesa. He could sober up and be ready for the race the next morning. My brother has never forgiven me for taking this roustabout to his home. He is a great sailor and valuable crew, but this was his last Ensenada Race with us. We would miss his wild stories. Randy and Rex kept us in stitches with their repertoire of endless jokes all through the race. However, Randy's antics caused us a lot of stress.

The next morning was clear and crisp. We were rarin' to go. As we motored out to the start line, I offhandedly told Bob a hot dinner awaited us when the sun went down. His protocol for the race included having prepared sandwiches that you could eat with one hand, while tending a sail or tiller with the other. I had made some scrumptious turkey noodle soup and put it in a gallon thermos, then hid it under the forward bunk. Bob responded, "No, we won't." He had found the thermos and taken the delicious soup off the boat to keep our vessel light. Bob knew this was excessive and compulsive. I shrugged my shoulders; our eyes met for an instant before the episode was forgotten.

What a blast it was cruising our boat among the other boats at the Ensenada Race official start line. It takes an hour to get all six-hundred-plus boats across the line, in a listed sequence. I was busy waving at friends on other boats and taking in the splendor. Our ten-minute warning gun went off, and serious racing maneuvers began. Bob had a good start, and we were on our way. Bill, Rex, Randy and I were sitting on the high side of the boat, trying to keep *Saltshaker* as flat in the water as possible. The wind was light, which helped us because our boat was a light-air screamer. We were nearing San Diego as the stars came out. In the dead of night, a large ketch-rigged motor-sailor was in the distance off our bow. As we gained on her, we saw an amazing sight. The guys on board were dressed in tuxedos. They were sitting around the large deck of their vessel smoking cigars and watching the movie *Deep Throat* being projected onto their mainsail. We knew we had now seen everything.

We sailed on through the night. Bob had chosen the right course. We hammered the competition. *Saltshaker* came in first in the MORF division.

A race official called Bob to the stage at the

|US Coast Guard admiral presenting Bob with the first-place trophy for the Midget Ocean Racing Fleet (MORF) division|

trophy presentation and presented him with a gargantuan perpetual trophy, given to him by an admiral in the US Coast Guard. Rex and I jumped up and cheered Bob, knocking Bill over in the process. Our spirits were high, and we were soaring above the clouds.

Later that summer, a new ultra-light sailboat came on the racing scene, and we were intrigued. We sold the twenty-nine-foot Ranger to a cardiologist in Los Angeles, who changed the name of the boat from *Saltshaker* to *Pacemaker*—the good doctor invented the pacemaker.

We heard about a one-off design twenty-four-foot Moore (a stripped-out ultralight racing machine) for sale in Santa Barbara. The hull was burgundy, with a beautiful spruce wooden deck, and no protruding cabin. Its freeboard was a skimpy twelve inches. The hull down below had no amenities, other than a race-required bunk, small stove, and sink. A bucket served as the head. We bought the boat, named it *Saltshaker*, raced it, and created a big ruckus. The local racers didn't think our little "gnat" boat should be out there racing against the bigger offshore racers (we beat the socks off of most of them).

Racing on a small nondisplacement ultralight was never relaxing. We were usually on the edge of crash and burn. Plowing through waves on our way to the weather mark, I sometimes looked up at the cockpit of larger displacement boats in the race with lots of freeboard and thought they looked relaxed and dry. However, I knew the excitement was the battle we were experiencing. Off-wind we surfed (displacement boats cannot surf), pumped the main for more speed, and hung on for the ride. Fast is fun had a new meaning.

Rex was in his last semester in high school and taking some college courses at Ventura Junior College. He had a gazillion girlfriends. Bob was winning more Ensenada races, participating in Trans-Pac Races, and rigging boats for customers. I was working at Petoseed Co. as an executive secretary to the CFO. Bill was working at Hughes Research in Santa Barbara. Life was busy. Most of our friends were sailors, and our activities, both social and sailing, revolved around local yacht clubs. I often thought we had a silver spoon in our mouths. We were lucky to have such a fun life, with many, many blessings.

The Santa Cruz Island Race was coming up on the race calendar. It is a seventy-mile race from Channel Islands Harbor, out around Santa Cruz Island, taking the island to port, then back to Channel Islands Harbor. On the Saturday morning of the race, it was cold and blustery, and we were short-crewed—we needed more weight on the weather rail. Bob, Rex, and I took off across the start line, for what was going to be an extreme ride in our little boat. *Saltshaker* was on its ear and rail-under heading into the wind. Bob fought the tiller to stay upright. The hull and most of the keel on the windward side was out of the water. It took most of the day to get close to the west end of the island. Huge waves picked our boat up, and we crashed down into the next wave. Rex and I were sitting on the rail, hanging on for dear life to the lifelines, getting blasted in the face with cold seawater. At one point I lifted my sailing boot up in the air, and a small fish fell out. I told the kids I knew this would be a wet ride, but I didn't think I needed my snorkel.

The wind was howling. Our mast was pumping, and the boat was shuttering on every mountainous wave. Water was cascading over the boat, as high as the spreaders. Bob steered *Saltshaker* as close to the island as possible to get protection from the wind. We were overpowered and needed to get the headsail down, but it was dicey. I, being the lightest, was the chosen one to go get the sail down. As I crawled along the deck, Rex held on to my ankles. Bob held onto Rex's ankles. The sail plummeted to the deck, as Bob tacked into the wind while letting the halyard go. We fought the sail when it started dragging in the water, lumbering to retrieve it and stuff it into the hatch. After a lot of grunting and groaning, the mission was accomplished.

The boat was now able to sail more upright, but we were not

making any headway. The west end of the island had no protection from a land mass—waves were mountainous. We knew it was dangerous to sail into the tumultuous waters that lay ahead. Our boat's twelve-inch freeboard was no match for the frenzied ocean we were trying to conquer.

Giving up and quitting a race is not easy, especially when we had come so far. For our safety and the boat's safety, we turned around. The ride back home was fast. The boat started surfing, blasting from one wave and onto another. The ocean was crazy. Nothing had broken on the boat, and we were fine. It was in the dead of night when Rex sighted the harbor entrance lights off in the distance. My boys and I gave each other high-fives.

After docking *Saltshaker* we took our exhausted bodies over to the yacht club to see how the race was going and if anyone else had quit. Bill, who was hanging around the yacht club anxiously waiting to hear any news about *Saltshaker*, told us several boats in the race had been dismasted.

All of the boats quit the race except for two, which happened to be captained by our fiercest competitors. We wanted to beat them in this race. Their win was hard to swallow. However, we congratulated both skippers and their crews on a great race, knowing their boats were lightning-fast and well sailed.

Bob's rigging business was getting established, and he was sailing on the "gold-plated racers." He proposed to his sweetheart, Sue, who Bob met through her dad, who sailed aboard our boat in various races. They were married in a formal church wedding ceremony. Bob asked Rex to be his best man. Both Bob and Rex wore identical suits. They were the same size now. I went to the beauty shop to get my hair done (for the first and only time in my life) and bought a new gown for the wedding. Bill looked snappy in his new suit. The bride wore a stunning white wedding gown. Our son was embarking on a new life.

A few days after the wedding, Bob left on the Los Angeles

to Manzanilla Sailboat Race. The honeymoon was a week in the exclusive beach resort town of Manzanilla, Mexico. Sue flew down to meet Bob at the finish line.

Bob was hugely excited about racing on the world-famous *Ragtime*, a sixty-eight-foot ultrafast yacht racer. He looked good behind the wheel, as the boat took off from the start line.

|Bob and crew racing to Mexico|

Rex drove over to the apartment Bob and Sue had rented to play a few tricks on the newlyweds. He took the labels off the food cans, TP'd the place, short sheeted the bed, and generally messed up their new home. That would give them a laugh when they returned from their honeymoon!

Rex's Death

A week after Bob left for Mexico on the sailboat race, Bill and I had a relaxing soak in the Jacuzzi and were starting to prepare dinner, waiting for Rex to appear through the door. We got a call from a person we didn't know who said Rex had been in an auto accident and was in St. John's Hospital. We drove to the hospital and were met at the door by a priest. Rex, who was two months shy of his eighteenth birthday, had died in the crash. It was February 19, 1978.

Our world was shattered. This kid lived life to the fullest. He was an excellent student, an up-and-coming sailboat racer, always jumped in to help whoever needed assistance, was a kick to be around, and pulled his weight in any situation. He was mature beyond his years and loved everyone, and everyone loved him. I didn't know if I could ever smile again, or stop crying.

Sue's father tried to contact Bob on *Ragtime* all night on a ship-to-shore radio. He finally reached the boat early the next morning. The crew did not tell Bob about his brother, because they were very close to the finish line, and they felt it better to wait until the boat had docked. Telling a mate that his brother had died must have been agonizingly difficult.

Bob and Rex were as close as brothers get. Rex had enormous self-confidence for his age. The boys sailed and surfed together, and Rex helped Bob in his rigging business.

To picture Bob jumping off the boat, sail bag in hand, climbing up the dock ramp to embrace his new wife, only to be met with the news of Rex's death tore my heart out.

We had Rex cremated and held a service for him at a mortuary in Oxnard. His friends were devastated, their emotions uncontrolled. I leaned heavily on Bill, my body shaking violently as we both sobbed.

Bill and I asked Bob not to come home from his honeymoon early. We waited for him to return before we scattered Rex's ashes at sea.

Mom and her husband lived in Atascadero. Friends drove them to our house. The sorrow we were going through, making funeral arrangements and notifying family, friends, coworkers, and Bob and Rex's friends, was amplified in Bob's broken voice when he called home from Mexico. The phone call was tough for all of us—, my husband Bill, Bob, and myself. Bob kept saying, "Please don't cry so hard, Mom."

Bill and I struggled through the next few days. The memorial service was an experience I wouldn't wish on my worst enemy. When Bob and Sue returned, Bob was my strength. The trip out to sea to scatter Rex's ashes was sad and extremely emotional for all of us. Bob wrote a poignant poem for Father James (the Episcopal priest at the parochial school where Rex was a student from kindergarten through fourth grade) to read during the service. This day was rugged. We felt empty inside.

I didn't want to go into the garage. Rex and Bob had both built themselves a bedroom by partitioning off part of the garage. Their surfboards hung on the wall next to each other. Instead of stomping of feet, voices, and the slamming of doors, there was silence.

Bill and I were a wreck.

It was absolutely necessary for the two of us to get our lives functioning again. We both went back to work.

Bob and Sue were trying to adjust to married life. For a lark, they interviewed for the *Newlywed Show* in Hollywood. They were chosen as participants. Sue was asked several questions about how Bob would answer questions. Bob was asked the same about Sue. When the show's host brought them together, and their answers were told to each other, it was obvious that they did not have a clue about how the other one thought.

Sue had a loss similar to Bob's. Her only brother was killed in an automobile accident two years before Rex's death. This double tragedy, plus differences in personalities, had an impact on their marriage. Several months after the wedding, Bob and Sue's marriage was annulled.

Our family was having a difficult time repairing itself. Bob continued sailing and working, and found a new girlfriend. Bill and I were trying to lead a normal life.

Approximately one year later, Bill and I were served with a lawsuit, which stated that the guy that owned the car that was involved in the accident with Rex was suing us for damages. We were stunned. How could this happen in a reasonable world?

The owner was not in the car. He lived in Beverly Hills, and the driver of his car was a lowlife on Silver-Strand Beach in Port Hueneme, who had run away from the accident scene. He was caught by the police a short time later because he had a scrape on his right knee. There was a bent panel in the car where the driver's knee slammed into it.

Rex was driving a VW Bug. In a head-on collision, a lightweight rear-engine car has no defense when a heavy-metal Detroit monster hits it. I don't know how much damage there was to the car because I never saw it after the accident. His body showed no sign of injury. The autopsy said he had died instantly from internal injuries.

First, we sought an attorney (our first experience with the legal system). After a consultation, the attorney said we needed to get an accident report from the police department and a verification of Rex's character and place in the community.

Letters were written by his adult sailing friends, school officials, the local Boys Club where Rex donated time teaching boys how to sail, the local yacht clubs, and his surfing buddies.

Bill and I made it clear to the attorney that we wanted to fight this lawsuit in a counterlawsuit, but did not want to go to court. It was emotionally dreadful to contemplate. We did not care about proceeds. When an out-of-court settlement was reached, our side won.

The driver of the car that hit Rex was seen in Port Hueneme wearing a voodoo doll around his neck to protect him from Rex's spirit.

My son's untimely death at age seventeen was a tragic waste of a beautiful life.

Our family recovered from Rex's death, but the sadness in our hearts will never cease. We forced ourselves to focus on future plans.

Bob's Single-Handed Trans-Pac Race

Bob had an extreme goal: sail from San Francisco, California, to Hanalei, Kauai, in the 1980, 2,300-mile Single-Handed Trans-Pac Race. Several sailboat races from the West Coast to Hawaii are crewed. This is the only race where one person races his or her boat alone across the Pacific Ocean.

Our son wanted to sail our twenty-four-foot Moore *Saltshaker* in the race. It was tough for Bill and me to encourage this decision because of the risk. Bob is a capable sailor and a strong person, both mentally and physically. He raced several long-distance single-handed races over a year's time to qualify for the Trans-Pac race.

One such race started in Los Angeles Harbor and went around San Nicolas Island—about one hundred miles out to sea. Bob told us about a storm that closed in on the racers, producing gale-force wind and huge waves. A loud bang startled him. He looked over the side of the boat. The hull had caved in but did not break. Bob continued on his course. The next big wave popped the side back out. He could see no damage to the hull and went on to win the race.

When the big day arrived to leave Channel Islands Harbor and head north, Bob secured *Saltshaker* on a trailer behind his truck. He drove to San Francisco so he could equip and ready her for the start of the Single-Handed Trans-Pac. About a week later, Bill and I drove up the coast to meet Bob at the St. Francis Yacht Club, the host yacht club for the race.

San Francisco Harbor was alive with boats sailing in and out of anchorages and out to the open sea. On the dock in front of the St. Francis Yacht Club, where all the Single-Handed Trans-Pac boats were lined up, ABC Television was interviewing Bob about the race and what his strategies were. His new girlfriend, Jill, was there too. Approximately forty boats, some from other countries, had entered the event.

Down below deck, in the minuscule cabin of *Saltshaker*, there were no amenities, just four plastic laundry baskets secured under the bow area with screws attached to the inside cabin top. Bob cut a door in the baskets and stored his clothes in one, foul weather gear in one, his food in another, and a foam-padded basket held his navigational gear.

One of the prerequisites of the race was to use only charts and a sextant—no other navigational equipment or electronic gear allowed. Bob had studied sextant navigation before he left and knew how to take sightings. He knew he had a lot to learn and was sure he could master the precision needed to take sightings in extreme weather conditions. The next point of land, if he missed the north end of Kauai, was Japan. An emergency encapsulated raft was lashed on deck. GPS was not available to the yachting community in 1980—no EPIRB, a locating device, either.

A gallon of gas to power the generator that recharged batteries for the self-steering mechanism was stowed down below on the cabin bulkhead. Bob also carried a one-hour egg timer to wake himself up in the middle of the night. The only communication equipment aboard was a battery-powered handheld radio with a range of about ten miles.

Our sailing friends Tim and Kathy and Jill joined us in San Francisco to see the start of the race. We watched as Bob left his slip in front of the St. Francis Yacht Club. His boat looked small among the other boats. Bob waved good-bye to us and headed out the channel to the start line, under the Golden Gate Bridge. What was going on in his head—the adventure, the unknown dangers, loneliness? Probably none of the above.

My heart was in my throat. It took all the courage I could muster to stand and cheer him on. Rex would have been proud of his brother.

When the start gun went off, the boats were crowding the start line and trying to get a "hot" start. In San Francisco Bay the tide is strong, and when the wind is light, the boats sometimes are pushed backward, which is why the boats were bunched together. Bob's boat hit the start-mark. He had to reround the mark.

Eight days later, Tim, Kathy, Jill, Bill, and I flew from LAX to Hawaii. The finish line was in Kauai, the most northern island in the chain of Hawaiian Islands.

We rented a condo on a cliff overlooking Hanalei Bay, the finish line. The five of us settled in for the anxious wait of sighting boats off the coast of Kauai. The first boat to finish the race was *Crusader* the only multihull in the race. The second boat was *Panish*, a fifty-five-foot racer. The skipper knew Bob well and said he had sighted him along the way (they had raced together on the crewed Trans-Pac from Los Angeles to Diamond Head). Bob had not seen *Panish* because the twenty-four-foot Moore has a low freeboard. That precluded him from sighting over the top of most waves.

On the fourteenth day of the race, Tim, Kathy, and Bill and I were standing on the pier looking out over Hanalei Bay. We spotted a little yellow sailboat blasting around the edge of the island and into the bay. The guy hunched over the tiller was Bob!

The race committee was in radio contact with him. Bob sailed toward the finish buoy, located in the middle of the bay. Jill had been hanging out at race committee headquarters and jumped in the race committee boat to go out and meet Bob.

After the race committee gave him the "finish" gun, they asked, "Do you want champagne or beer?" Bob took the champagne and pointed at Jill.

The jubilant couple sailed into Hanalei Bay anchorage, and I thought they would never drop a hook. We waved frantically from the pier. Finally, the two of them dropped anchor and took the mainsail down—all the while completely involved with each other, not noticing us. I finally couldn't stand it anymore and dove off the end of the pier and swam over to the boat. I drank some of their champagne, but I don't think they even knew I was aboard *Saltshaker*. The hatch boards were in. I swam back to the pier so we could drive down to the beach in front of where the boat was anchored.

A big welcome cheer went up when we spotted two souls dive into the water off the bow of Saltshaker and swim to shore. Bob was thin. He had lost over twenty pounds. Stories of the race came slowly, in Bob's own time. He had sores all over his body from wearing wet foul-weather gear. He said it was cold and rainy the whole way, except for the last three days.

Bob described one incident that sounded scary as hell: "On a cold, rainy night, about halfway through the race, the wind was howling and the boat was pitching wildly. The spinnaker was wrapped around the head stay. I climbed the mast. I couldn't hang on, fell, and hit the spinnaker pole, breaking it in half. I fell to the deck with the torn spinnaker. Hitting the pole saved me from going overboard."

Luckily, Bob carried an extra spinnaker pole. He was also able to sew the sail back together.

There were many anxious moments in the race, and I asked Bob if he cussed a lot. He replied, "No, Mom, I wanted to be on the side of the Lord." I had never known Bob to be particularly religious before this.

The food and water supply he carried on the race had dwindled to one pack of freeze-dried peas and a pint of water. Bob needed to inflate his emergency raft to get at the rations inside, if he had not finished the race when he did.

Saltshaker took first place in the ultralight division and second place overall in the race. The Single-Handed Society threw awesome luaus after the boats finished. I danced the hula before an audience of single-handed sailors at one of the affairs, with a Hawaiian band playing in the background.

Our group was now in full-on vacation mode. During the day we bodysurfed the waves along the Hanalei Bay shore line.

As the afternoon breeze picked up, Bob, Jill, and I were on the lookout for a party boat. Once spotted, we swam out, and climbed aboard. We were always welcomed with open arms.

"Spinnaker flying" was the best game in town. The "flyer" stands on the bow of the sailboat and sits down in a bosun's chair, which is attached to the lines coming off a voluminous spinnaker sail. It was my turn. A gust of wind picked up the spinnaker. The flight began. I was hoisted into the air, out in front of the anchored boat. Being a lightweight, the spinnaker flew me as high as the spreaders. When the gust let up, the spinnaker collapsed, and I was dunked into the ocean. Everyone on the boat took turns; laughter and chaotic behavior was paramount.

Trade winds blow a constant twenty to twenty-five knots in the afternoon, making this sport a great challenge. There were many boats with fifty to eighty-foot masts anchored in the harbor, waiting for anyone willing to "spinnaker fly."

Early in the morning in Hanalei, if the clouds do not cover the top of the mountains in the distance (signaling a dry day), it's time to go hiking into the jungles of the Na Pali coastline. The hike is awesomely beautiful, but the rocky footpath along the coastal cliffs is slippery, even without rain, and downright soggy if it is raining. This is one of the wettest places on earth, with over six hundred inches of rain per year.

We woke to a cloudless day, packed some granola bars and water, and drove to the end of Hanalei Road where the hiking trail begins. Once we hiked over the rocky Na Pali coast cliff area, we reached the open beach. This beach is one of the most beautiful I have ever seen. There are rocky caves in the green and lush cliffs. The ocean is emerald green, and small waves roll into the protected white-sand beach. Outer clothes were dumped on the rocks, and we ran through the sand into the sea. This must be heaven.

Hiking boots and shirts back on, we turned toward the mountains and started picking our way through thick jungle. Our goal was to reach the legendary Hanakapiai Falls. It was difficult hiking, and there was no trail (sometimes a rock, wrapped in toro leaves, pointed the way across a stream). We were lucky—we spotted the imposing falls through a hole in the treetops.

Once we reached the falls, Bob, Jill, Tim, and I dove into the freezing pool of water at the bottom of the falls and swam back behind the cascading water. We found out later how dangerous it was to swim around the three-hundred-foot falls. Rocks and coconuts can roll off the top. Luckily, no one got clunked in the head. The jungle and surrounding steep cliffs cause long shadows in the afternoon. Everyone was cold and wet, so we scrambled through the wild landscape to where the beach reached the ocean, which was drenched in warm sunshine. By this time we were hungry and in a hurry to climb back over the Na Pali coastline to reach a little trailer hut on the Hanalei River. This is where tropical tacos are sold. We made it back in time. The owner of this business closes up when the surf is up. After purchasing some cold beer and delicious tropical tacos, we sat on the grass by the gentle flowing Hanalei River's edge, knowing what sublime contentment is.

Another famous waterfall is well known to the locals. It is in a little town a few miles south of Hanalei. We drove there and started our search for the hidden falls. A fenced-off area was suspect. I started to climb over the fence, and just as I was on top of the fence, a sheriff pulled up in his pickup truck. He yelled, "Can't you read?" I looked below me and noticed a big red sign that said "KEEP OFF." I climbed down and apologized to the officer.

Our group drove off in the car, went around the block, and came across an old boatyard, looked around, then spotted two kids with towels over their shoulders, and quickly followed them into a dense forest of lush trees. Soon, we could hear the roar of a big waterfall. The locals told us this waterfall was used in the movie *South Pacific*. They also told us you could ride the waterfalls down to the pool of water below and climb the rocks along the edge of the waterfall, back to the top. This was *it*!

We spent hours getting squirted off the top of the falls and diving off the rocks. This was my lifetime dream, playing Tarzan— jumping and screaming through the waterfalls and then doing a swan dive off the rocks, just like Esther Williams did in her beautiful and romantic swimming films.

Tim and I took Bob's boat out of Hanalei Harbor for a sail one afternoon. Dolphins danced in front of the boat while we crashed through the waves. The seas, wind, and magnificent coastal mountains all contributed to a stellar day at sea. When we returned from the sail, Bill was on the beach waiting for us, and he was pissed. I had asked Bill if he wanted to go sailing, but he was being a grump and said no.

It was time to return to the mainland and go back to work.

Divorce from Bill Boyes

Bill's possessiveness had intensified after we lost Rex. Sitting down together after work with a glass of wine became the important part of the day for Bill. This drove me nuts. Alcohol and negativity was not productive therapy for either of us. Bill was pulling me in, and I wanted to break out. I felt most free when I was running on the beach. It was there that I felt closest to Rex. We had scattered his ashes out to sea, in line with Santa Cruz and Anacapa Islands. When I ran along the beach, looking out across the water, I felt a sadness but had a carefree spirit within my soul.

It is said that after losing a child, you and your spouse are either drawn together or torn apart. The latter happened to Bill and me. Rex would not have wanted either of us to stop living life to the fullest because of our grief over his death.

After almost twenty-five years of marriage, raising two children, having a typical happy family life, and then having the wind taken out of our sails, I decided to end our marriage. I could see nothing holding it together.

Bob and Jill had stayed in Hawaii with the boat after the single-handed race. They sailed *Saltshaker* from Kauai to Oahu to set up a rigging business in the harbor.

I was taking some business courses after work at Laverne University at the Point Mugu Naval Base in Port Hueneme, just south of Oxnard.

I knew that Bill did not want to live by himself and that leaving him meant I needed to try to find my replacement. Luckily, there was a friendly lady psychiatrist who lived in our condo complex. We talked with her in the Jacuzzi and even went skiing together in Colorado. As the friendship grew, I noticed her attraction to Bill.

When Bill realized our marriage was over, he became involved with the psychiatrist. I came home from school one evening, and Bill was not there. He stayed all night with her.

The next day, I went to the courthouse on my lunch break from work and obtained the papers necessary to start divorce proceedings. It cost forty dollars to file the paperwork. I wrote a divorce contract agreement that split everything Bill and I owned equally. We had a pretrial hearing in which the judge signed our agreement on January 15, 1981. Our divorce would be final in six months. No attorneys were needed.

Bob and Jill decided to come back to California. Since *Saltshaker* was too tiny to sail to weather from Hawaii back across the Pacific Ocean to California, we had to find a way to ship the boat home. I was working for a horticultural company that had nurseries in Oahu. Once in a while plants from the Oahu nursery were shipped back to our Southern California facility. Luckily, my boss was able to arrange for our boat to be loaded into a scheduled shipment. Inside the container, vegetable plants were stacked around our little twenty-four-foot boat and loaded onto a freighter.

I felt terrible when I told Bob that Bill and I were getting a divorce. He had lost his brother, and now his mom and dad were splitting up. To my relief, Bob was understanding and supportive of my decision. He said: "Mom, I'll probably have more moms and dads to love, because I believe both of you will remarry." Bob never took sides in the divorce, and I did not talk negatively about Bill to him.

Bill told me I would fail in my quest to start a new life. He believed that I was not strong enough to endure single life and that I would never be able to support myself, let alone keep the condo we owned in Channel Islands Harbor.

In a very generous proposal my brother gave me a loan to pay Bill for his portion of our home equity, so I was able to continue to live in my condo.

I had confidence I could succeed. My health was good, and my body was strong. Also, I had a job that was covering the cost of my brother's loan, mortgage payments and household expenses. I cut my spending to the bone.

Politics were not in the forefront and had taken a backseat to the transformations that beset our family. In spite of that, consequential national and international incidents were affecting America.

The Cold War

The world was being engulfed in a daring duel of ideologies between the two countries that had done the most to win World War II—the Soviet Union and the United States. The conflict between the world's two new superpowers stopped short of all-out war and became the Cold War. Nuclear confrontation and devastation were too gruesome for the two countries to contemplate. Instead, each sought to outflank and destabilize the other.

Ronald Reagan won a landslide victory in the 1980 presidential election. As a kid I watched a young Reagan in idealistic western movies. In 1967 I listened to him campaigning for governor of California at a rally in Thousand Oaks. He won and served as our governor until 1974.

On the sixty-ninth day of his presidency, Reagan was shot in the chest by another would-be presidential assassin. The president was wounded but recovered quickly.

During Reagan's presidency, he cut taxes while dramatically

increasing defense spending. Savings and loan institutions and other financial institutions were deregulated. This caused the late 1980s savings and loan institution debacle under Charles Keating.

The president introduced SDI (Strategic Defense Initiative)—a space-based antimissile defense system—to confront what he labeled the USSR's "evil empire."

In a gesture of peace, Reagan signed the INF (Intermediate-Range Nuclear Forces) Treaty with Soviet President Mikhail Gorbachev. It limited intermediate-range missiles and cut stockpiles of nuclear weapons by 20 percent—not enough but a start.

Gorbachev introduced glasnost (openness) in the Soviet Union and pressed Eastern bloc allies to do the same. Massive demonstrations on both sides of the Berlin Wall brought about the collapse of the East German government. Simultaneous demonstrations ended Communist rule in Czechoslovakia and Bulgaria. Within the next year, the Communist Party was disbanded. Poland, Albania, and Estonia moved toward democracy.

Twenty-four years after Kennedy's visit to Berlin, as tensions between the two superpowers eased, President Ronald Reagan made an appearance at the Berlin Wall. He spoke passionately about the advance of human liberty and challenged Soviet leader Mikhail Gorbachev to "tear down this wall," the ultimate symbol of Communist oppression. In 1989 the Berlin Wall fell, signaling the end of the Cold War.

Reagan served two terms as president, and enjoyed every minute of it, along with his wife, Nancy, who still lovingly calls him Ronnie.

He retired to his vast horse ranch in the Santa Barbara mountains, but Reagan was suffering from Alzheimer's, and his health deteriorated to the point he was incapacitated and unable to enjoy the richness of his retirement. He was, and still is, a beloved president.

CHAPTER 5

Single Life; Triathlons

Fling

Change has always been easy for me, whether it's moving to a new city or changing jobs. Losing Rex was a noxious change. Ending a marriage certainly is emotionally upsetting, but I felt the change was necessary to get out of the doldrums of being in a confined marriage. As this chapter of my life closed, my mind was focused forward not back.

I was racing into uncharted territory. I married Bill when I was nineteen years old. Now, in my late forties, life was different—women were stepping out, becoming business professionals, and demanding autonomy. Freedom from the phrase "women's place in society" meant that there were no longer any constraints—women had unlimited aspirations to pursue their dreams.

In July of 1982, I decided to go to Hawaii with my friend Debbie to view the finish of the Los Angeles to Diamond Head Trans-Pac Sailboat Race. Bob had been hired to race a fifty-two-foot carbon fiber boat.

Our airline flight across the Pacific was a crack-up. Debbie and I hit the bar at the airport and had a glow going when we boarded our flight. When the stewardess came down the aisle to ask us what we wanted to drink, we both ordered two Bloody Marys and told the guy who was sitting in between us that he better order a couple of drinks also. The movie started to play and I fell asleep. When I woke up, there was no Debbie. She had gone to the bathroom and then took a nap. The stewardess woke her up, and Debbie came down the aisle laughing. When the flight landed, we were still pretty buzzed. The guy that was sitting in between us had gotten with the program, and we all three swerved down the steps of the airplane and out onto the tarmac at the Oahu airport. Debbie and her husband have a lot of friends on the island. A few of them picked us up at the airport in a limo, putting leis around our necks (much kissing and hugging), then gave us Mai Tais to drink during our ride through Waikiki. We were staying on a fancy powerboat in Ala Moana Harbor. The party lasted another two weeks.

Debbie and I were invited aboard various boats that powered out to the Diamond Head finish line to escort the Trans-Pac racers into Ala Moana Harbor. This routine went on all day and night, as each boat finished. Bob's boat finished in the middle of the day. I heard the loudspeaker announce his name and the rest of the crew's names as the boat turned the corner of the yacht club to tie up in their appointed slip. Our friend Dave was skippering a Japanese boat. He finished in the middle of the night. The ocean was rough and the wind was screaming, but we managed to toss him some champagne at the Diamond Head finish line from our power boat.

The sponsors of the finishing boat, usually local Hawaiian families, were alerted their boat had finished the race and the boat was sailing from Diamond Head toward the marina. The job of the sponsor was to bring Mai Tais, pupus, and fresh flower leis aboard the finishing boat—and let the party begin!

We did not miss any of the nightly luaus at yacht clubs around the island. A final trophy presentation at the fancy Ala Moana

Hotel on Waikiki Beach was an absolute blast. I sat at the table with Bob's boat owner and crew. They had their first-place trophy setting in the middle of the table. About midnight, the whole place was rockin'. A decision to sail to Hanalei Bay, Kauai, was made. We all decided that was a fine idea, so I said good-bye to Debbie and the gang, jumped aboard the boat and sailed away into the night.

The next morning, we reached our destination. Numerous waterfalls were visible, with the lush rolling green mountains of the Na Pali coast bathed in the early-morning sun. We sailed into this island paradise. I was mesmerized by the beauty. One aspect spoiled the picture. Bill and his new bride were honeymooning on the island. Boy, were they upset when they found out I was on the boat.

I decided it best if I fled the scene. I took an interisland flight to the pineapple island of Lanai. A bunch of my sailing friends were there. When the small plane landed on the Lani airstrip, a special friend, Captain Jim, played his trumpet as I danced down the ramp. The next week we hiked, dove for fish off the coast, got to know the natives on the island, and got little rest between gatherings. The Pineapple Isle Yacht Club was born and christened with uproarious enthusiasm by celebrating sailors and local pineapple pickers on a beach near the Lani Harbor. Hawaiian dancers and musicians brought friendship and a party atmosphere to the festivities. We ate a pig that was roasted underground and devoured an array of scrumptious food and drink. The yacht club burgee has, of course, a big pineapple in the middle of the pennant.

The return flight home was much quieter. When Debbie and I returned to California, she took my picture as I fell, dog tired, across my suitcase in the airport parking lot. The flowered lei I had around my neck had been crumpled into a deplorable mess. Facing humdrum issues at home sucked.

I joined three ski clubs. This turned out to be my salvation. My married friends were not keen on having a single woman in their midst. Besides, they were a little too sedate for me. I started snow skiing with my newfound ski club friends, running in 10k races, kayaking, hiking, and sailboat racing, and was still working as an administrative assistant at a vegetable seed company. My life during the early 1980s was frenzied.

Rob was my kayak buddy. On many evenings after work he and I paddled out to the middle of Channel Islands Harbor to set off fireworks in front of the Whales Tail Restaurant. The Harbor Patrol shut us down, so we paddled out beyond the breakwater and into the ocean to set off rockets and pyrotechnics.

Rob helped me shoot out lights mounted to the roof of the mushroom-shaped tower across from my two-story condo. The lights shined into my bedroom and were distracting. I climbed to the top of the tower, hung out various windows, and tried repositioning the lights upward, downward, and sideways. It did not fix the problem. Rob had an air rifle. When it was foggy and dark outside, I called and asked him to come over with his rifle. We stood right underneath the light, Rob quickly pumped the gun to get good pressure and shot it. We ran like hell, each in opposite directions, as the glass from the spotlight came tinkling down the side of the building. We repeated this nonsense several times. Years later I found out that we had been seen by one of the homeowners' board of directors.

Snow skiing came easy, and on my first ski club trip to Mammoth Mountain, California, I noticed that all the guys were skiing down the slope from the top of the mountain. The gals were not as aggressive, messing around on the bottom of the slope. I was determined to become a good skier, not only because I enjoyed skiing with the guys, but it was a real rush to point the skies over the lip of a steep cliff and let 'em go! Ski clubs sponsor ski racing. It is a big part of their club persona. I am competitive, so ski racing was a natural progression. The excitement and challenge of racing was fun. I put my full energy into trying to keep upright on my skis while charging through the gates.

A National Ski Week was held during January of 1983 in Crested Butte, Colorado. Ski clubs across the United States participate in vying for top racing honors for their club. I flew to Colorado with the Los Padres Ski Club, out of Ventura, to race on Mount Crested Butte with unknown competition. I signed up for the women's dual slalom races. I found it fairly easy to intimidate other racers. Standing at the gate, with ski tips out over the mountain as far as I could get them, while firmly planted in a strong push-off position, I looked over at my competition and gave a nod of the head. This seemed to freak out the person I was racing against. Self-confidence brings success. Guess what—I won three gold medals! Our club did very well in the overall competition, and we celebrated mightily at the trophy presentation.

God was not a part of my life. I selfishly tended to my own needs, rarely saw Bob or my mom, partied a lot, drank too much, and was arrested for drunk driving. Being small in stature, it didn't take much to get me tipsy. The police caught me while driving erratically down the road after a ski club social event.

Drunk-driving school was poignant. My son Rex was killed by a drunk driver. I sat through the class thoroughly disgusted with myself.

Profligate actions on my part were about to ruin my life, if I didn't break the cycle. I decided to stop drinking and bring myself out of camp-run-amuck.

Becoming an Athlete

Running and biking became priorities after work and on weekends. Adding to this schedule, I began swimming laps with local swim clubs at Ventura College. This led to participating in triathlons and marathons. The regimentation helped me become healthier and stronger. It also gave my life focus.

Turning fifty was a big deal for me, and I wanted to do something special where I celebrated all year. I threw myself a birthday party at my condo and announced to my friends that I had chosen to train for the 1985 Ironman World Championship Triathlon in Kona, Hawaii. The race was one year away. This was a serious decision. Now my credibility was on the line.

Inner strength, toughness, hard work, and confidence are needed to accomplish important achievements. While growing up, I did not understand the importance of pushing myself to greater heights. The task that lay before me required me to toughen up, both mentally and physically.

Enthusiasm is a tough thing to hang onto. Frittering away valuable time does not "get 'er done," as my son Bob is fond of saying.

It would take total dedication to accomplish my goal of not only finishing the race, but doing well and, if extremely lucky, medaling in this event. Athletes swim 2.5 miles in the open ocean, bike 112 miles over the hilly and hot windy course that winds its way through Kona's lava beds, then run a marathon (26.2 miles), pounding their bodies in the tropical heat. This is not for wimps! I had to be ultraregimented and passionate about my training.

An Ironman training camp was held in Kona in October. I signed up for it. My two-week vacation from work was spent learning firsthand from expert trainers how to become a successful triathlete. This was a high intensity two-week workout, held at the Kona Hilton. We learned about proper diet and our body-fat content and had extensive training from swim, biking, and running coaches. At the conclusion of the training camp, we were transported around the race course during the 1984 Ironman. This allowed us fledgling athletes to learn the magnitude of each segment of the race.

During the next year I competed in nine triathlons, wining every one in my age category. I qualified for the Ironman by winning the Santa Barbara Half Distance Ironman Triathlon. This provided me with the knowledge that I was accepted into the race, so it was full steam ahead!

I competed in the 1985 LA Triathlon Championship and was tied for first place in the Master's Cup (age forty and over). The year before, I had won the Master's Cup. This was a sprint triathlon, consisting of a half-mile swim, ten-mile bike race, and six-mile run. When I got in the water for the final triathlon in the series, the race officials announced my name, along with the professional triathletes. I was stoked.

The swim went great, and I was ahead in my age group until the end of the bike race, when I spun out on a sharp corner of the road that was covered with sand. I had come into the bike-run transition area too fast. My bike and I fell to the ground. I knew I had sustained road rash in the crash, but I got up off the asphalt and tried to climb back on my bike. It collapsed under me, because the wheel was broken in four places. A race attendant ran over and took the bike, so I could continue to the transition area and change from my biking shoes to my running shoes. I could feel a lot of ooze down my arms and legs, but the rest of my body seemed to be working. I took off on the run and got a lot of strange looks on the course. Many runners passed me. I had lost my first-place lead but managed a second overall in the series. When I crossed the finish line, a race attendant asked if he could help me to the first aid station. I thanked him and said I could manage okay. I spent the next hour having my wounds washed out. After the medical crew bandaged my injuries, I hobbled over to the trophy presentation and received a second-place medal. I had lost the race, and my ego was wounded.

When I drove back to Channel Islands Harbor, I decided to drop my racing wheel off at the local bike shop to be repaired, because I was scheduled to compete in another race in two weeks. Bob happened to go into the bike shop the next day to get some parts for his bike and saw my wheel hanging over the repair shop counter. He said, "Boy, what happened to the person that did that?" The bike store owner told Bob whose wheel it was and that I had been involved in a crash. I know I caused Bob a lot of anguish during my single years.

After taking some aspirin when I got home, I called my doctor friend, Sam, and told him of my plight. He asked how long it had been since I had a tetanus shot. I couldn't remember, so he came over to give me a shot. When Sam walked into the door, he took one look at me and said, "Do you have a scrub brush?" I thought I was going to faint! He said the abrasions will marbleize unless you get all the sand and gravel washed out.

For the next two weeks I sat on the very edge of my chair at work and had to stay out of the pool. Every place on my arms and legs that had gotten damaged leaked gooey ooze until they finally scabbed over.

I had never run a marathon. It was time. There was a Fiesta Marathon in Phoenix, which my friend John encouraged me to enter. He was running the marathon also. We stayed at the beautiful Camelback Hotel. The next morning, at pre-dawn, we climbed aboard a bus that shuttled us 26.2 miles out of town.

When we arrived at the start line, we saw runners huddled over fires that had been lit to keep all the skinny non-body-fat marathoners warm. Some runners were putting petroleum jelly on their bodies in places that I never thought to put the grease. As the sun came up, we gathered at the start line; the gun went off, and we were gone.

The winding road took us through mountainous desert terrain before we entered population centers on the edge of town. I had heard that most runners hit the wall at about the twenty-mile mark. That is when all the nourishment in our bodies has been used up, and the body starts feeding on itself. It was about this point in the race that a spectator had a radio along the curbside playing the song "Chariots of Fire." I straightened my shoulders, held my head high, and carried that song to the finish line.

Our group of friends gathered in the hotel's Jacuzzi after the race to celebrate our feat. That evening we ate heartily and danced the night away. My first experience of running a marathon was stupendous!

I was hot to trot and feeling my oats. John had qualified to run the Boston Marathon. There was an upcoming marathon qualifier in San Diego. I signed up for it. John told me that if I qualified, he would take me to Boston to run in this prestigious race, and we would see the city. Hot diggedy damn!

My training was going well, but a week before the marathon I came down with an awful cold that settled in my chest. John drove me to San Diego. He ran the first few miles with me and thought I was going to be all right. I was holding my eight-minute mile, which was needed to qualify for Boston. About halfway into the race, I started to crap out. My pace slowed dramatically. Taking a deep breath was impossible. I was able to finish, walking the last eight miles, but failed to achieve my goal. I held back tears all the way home in the car. To console me, John took me to dinner at a wonderful restaurant in Ojai where we sat in a hot tub before getting a massage and having a fine dinner.

Ironman Triathlon

When I was training for the Ironman I taped a scrap of paper to my wallet that reads:

To achieve goals, they must be realistic.

Remain focused—work hard.

Alter course when necessary.

Be responsible, positive-minded, and considerate of others.

WHEN ALL ELSE FAILS, TRY DOING IT WELL.

Every time I took my wallet out I read my creed and tried to concentrate on my lack of attention to detail, figuring out what corrective action was needed.

Formulating, and rigidly following, a meaningful and well-thought-out training schedule for the Ironman was imperative. I made up a weekly schedule of my workout and posted it on the refrigerator and bedroom doors. It changed with my level of training. Basically, the program was: get up at 4:30 a.m. and run eight miles on the beach before work; at lunch I walked around the outside of the building I worked in and lifted weights over my head for twenty minutes; after work I either biked forty miles around the agriculture fields of Oxnard or swam four thousand yards in the local college pool; Saturdays I competed in a triathlon or ran twenty miles; Sundays I biked at least one hundred miles—always somewhere where it was hilly, and hopefully, windy and hot, working hard to learn aerodynamics so I could compete with bigger and stronger triathletes.

All of this training was solo because, obviously, no one else was interested in self-inflicted pain. However, I had one friend, Rick, who occasionally biked with me on the weekend. After our ride I popped a big bowl of popcorn, which we ate while we floated the bowl in the Jacuzzi. Rick always brought an old dead chicken to barbecue for dinner.

My social life tanked because I needed my sleep; however, there was a great support group of friends who gave me encouragement. One of the main criteria of my preparation for the Ironman was to train smart and not get injured. I lucked out on this score, and my training peaked at the right time.

The weather is a giant factor in the Ironman Race. I flew to Hawaii two weeks prior to the race to train on the course and to get acclimatized. This was a good decision because I bonked on the bike course the first time I tried to ride it. I hadn't taken enough water or food, and my feet sweated so much in my bike shoes that they were swollen and sore, so I slit the top of my shoes to give me more room inside and got some Speedo pads to cushion the bottom of my feet.

A couple of guys from Europe were staying in the same condo complex. I met them in the Jacuzzi one evening. They told me they put lettuce on top of their heads, underneath their helmets, to keep cool in the blistering heat. They also said they put a piece of cow's liver in their pants to help cushion their junk from getting numb.

It took me a week to be able to run effectively on the course, and I jumped in the ocean every day to swim part of the course. There were stinging jellyfish to distract swimmers, and some days the water was as rough as the inside of a washing machine. The swim portion of the race is my weakest event, so I was intimidated by the course that went from the Kona pier out into the ocean 1.25 miles, around a sixty-foot catamaran, and then back to shore.

A few days prior to the race my friends, Ron and Brenda, and Jim and Ann, showed up in Kona. This was a terrific boost to my psyche. I had three professional massages during this time and cut way back on my training.

We even took time to venture down into a lava tube near Black Sands Beach, on the volcano side of the island (this famous beach was covered up by lava during an eruption a few years later). A local Hawaiian led us to a massive banyan tree and said, "We will climb down the roots of the tree. The lava tube below is a spiritual cave. Be respectful." Beside the tree we saw a hole in the ground. We edged ourselves down into the hole, trying to avoid the giant ants crawling around us. The water was about a foot deep at the bottom. We shined lights on the sides of the cave we were entering. Dirt ledges held Hawaiian ceremonial artifacts. I spotted melted candles, wooden bowls, and a skull. The water became warmer and deeper as we disappeared farther into the cave. It seemed like a good idea to hold hands in the darkness. We ventured farther into the lava tube. Waves pounded in the distance. The Hawaiian escorting us said, "Time to go back."

My marathon friend, John, arrived at the Kona Airport. He had done the Ironman two years before, and had placed second in his age group. John is a close friend. We sat out on the patio of my rented condo, sipping a fruit drink and watching the birds and flowers that framed the ocean landscape. He casually asked how much my preparation expenses leading up to the Ironman were. I thought about my custom racing bike, clothing, and travel during the last year and came up with an estimate. John wrote out a check for that amount and gave it to me. I was stunned by this generous gift and extremely grateful.

The night before the race, all I could hear was the roaring ocean and breaking surf. There was a hurricane offshore that caused a big buildup of frothy waves. I lay there hugging John tightly, planning my course of action for the swim.

A Chinese proverb states, "The mightiest oak in the forest is just a little nut that has held its ground."

Being a woman of small stature has not kept me from doing most anything a man can do. Strength-wise, I cannot compete.

The next morning in the predawn stillness, John and I walked down to the start area near the pier, my swim cap and goggles in hand. First, I went over and checked out my swim/bike transition area—bike tires pumped hard, helmet and biking shoes laid out neatly. It was time to step in the water. There were pops of bike tires exploding in the otherwise solemn morning air. Overzealous triathletes were overfilling their tires.

John gave me a hug and a "good luck, Sal." I descended the ladder going from the pier into the ocean with a slew of other wide-eyed triathletes. Suddenly, the magnitude of the event I was about to participate in hit me full-force. A lot of emotions welled up: excitement, apprehension, awe, and determination.

Participants must qualify for the event by winning an Ironman distance race in their age category, or a half Ironman. A few are pulled into the race by a lottery. The athletes come from around the world.

All are serious and well trained. The biggest segment is eighteen-to thirty-year-old males. Only 20 percent of the participants were women the year I competed. The rules of the race dictate that you must finish each segment of the race in a specified time: two hours for the swim, ten hours for the bike race, and six hours for the run. If you do not finish any segment within the time limit, you are pulled from the competition. The cutoff time for completion of the Ironman is midnight. In 1985 and for several years after, getting assistance from anyone during the race meant instant disqualification.

My well-thought-out strategy of getting away from the main throng of swimmers, who were strong young males capable of swimming over the top of me and making me lose my swim goggles, went right out the window. The waves were huge. I was getting washed back into the Kona Harbor break-wall. Out of nowhere, two gargantuan guys were on either side of me holding my shoulders down so I didn't get washed around. One of them looked down on me and said, "You gotta be the littlest person in this whole triathlon." I shot back at him, "I don't want any short jokes this morning." The three of us stood there among 1,100-plus other triathletes, swim goggles on our forehead, laughing, as the start gun went off.

I hurriedly pulled my goggles down over my eyes and dove among the sea of bodies around me—gone was my apprehension of getting clobbered by the powerful kicking of water polo players.

The big waves had a buffeting effect. The ocean was a confused mess. I swam as hard as I could through the water, propelled by the thought that I was doin' it!

The large catamaran sat at anchor at the turnaround point. When I reached this halfway point in the swim, I felt like the whale Ahab was tied to, peering up with one eye as I swam around the boat, looking at the spectators and photographers on the catamaran. After completing the turn, huge waves blocked any view of the shoreline, so I followed the swim caps of swimmers ahead of me. I learned later that several swimmers became seasick. When I approached the finish, I spotted swimmers around me, so I dove underneath the water and beat out three of them. Eric Heiden, the gold medalist speed skater (you know, the guy with thunder thighs) was the official clocking off the triathletes' numbers as we exited the water. I heard him yell out "1136"—my numbers. John was standing next to Heiden, cheering and clapping. My swim time was one hour and forty minutes.

I was exuberant running through the freshwater hoses overhead and into the transition area to get my bike gear. The officials were trying to calm the pack: "Take your time, and relax." *Relax? This is a race!* I pulled on my bike shorts, shoes, and helmet, and climbed aboard my bike, while running full speed, and rode off in a torrent of other bikers. We raced up the first hill. What lay before us was a long and grueling ride through the lava beds of the Kona coast, heading into the wind, toward the little town of Havii, the halfway turnaround spot, fifty-six miles north.

An aid station every five miles along the bike route gave out treats. Approaching the area, volunteers called out: "Banana, guava sandwich, cookies, water, Exceed?" Another volunteer

|*Exiting Ironman swim.*|

down the line had your request in their outstretched arm as you biked by so racers didn't have to slow down. At one aid station I called out "cookies." Next thing I knew—wham! I grabbed the bag as the guy shoved it into my outstretched hand, and cookie crumbs filled my bike glove.

Conscious of the dangerous effects that dehydration had on athletes performing in extreme heat while racing ultradistances, I devoured twenty-one pints of water and electrolyte fluid on the bike/run segments.

I had no idea how I was doing with my competition, but I was pedaling with all my might, except for getting off the bike three times to take a leak, because the importance of keeping hydrated had been hammered into my head. (I soon learned it was foolish to get off my bike to take a leak—just do as the guys do; move your bike pants aside and go.) Everything felt right, and I figured I was doing okay.

To my surprise, Ron, Brenda, Jim, Ann, and John had driven around the other side of the island (the Queen's Highway was closed to unofficial traffic) to greet me. One of them yelled, "You better put the pedal to the metal; you're in seventh place." That demoralized me. I started counting my blessings at that point—so far, I had not had a flat or other malfunction on my bike, and I felt good. Now I had better concentrate on keeping aerodynamic and trying to pass other bikers. I pedaled my fool head off, passing other bikers. As I neared the finish line, I knew the last hill was a killer, so I psyched myself up for the climb—no big deal—I nailed it. The bike ride took me a little under eight hours.

At the run transition station, the race officials again tried to get everyone to take their time and be calm. I did not take their advice! I threw on my running shorts, which had a picture of my sailboat painted on them by a friend of Bob's, changed shoes, and was off on my third and last segment of the Ironman.

A lot of other runners were around me, so I felt I was still in the mix of the pack. Running past the condo where John and I were staying, there were my friends jumping up and down and giving me encouragement.

My strategy was to walk up the hills and through the aid stations, which were placed at each mile point on the marathon course. I felt way too good to walk the hills and didn't slow down much at the aid stations. The route took us back out onto the Queen's Highway, to the airport turnoff road, which was the halfway mark of the marathon.

I was passing quite a few people. While passing two young guys who were struggling along, I tapped them on the butt and said, "Come on; pick it up." I was having a good time.

As darkness fell over the race course, aid station attendants passed out light sticks to the runners. There are no streetlights on the highway. Runners coming the other way were not visible—just jumping light sticks. We all poured water over our heads from the aid stations and gulped down what we could while running down the road. I was passing runners who were limping or had stomach cramps. I thanked the Lord that I was still able to compete.

Approaching town, I could hear the roar of the crowd at the finish line. I headed down the last hill and turned the corner to witness rows of people on bleachers, with flags waving and flowers everywhere, all cheering each athlete as they passed. Jim came out into the road and tried to take my picture as I passed. He said, "Slow down, Sal, so I can get your picture." Yeah, right! I crossed the finish line at thirteen hours, forty-seven minutes, taking third place in the fifty and over category of the women's division. Out of the 1,150 participants, I finished 600th, beating out several hundred young bucks!

Exuberance had a new meaning to me. The race officials placed an orchid lei around my neck and guided me to the medical tent. It looked like a scene out of *M*A*S*H*. I breezed through, hardly looking at those needing medical assistance.

Next stop was the massage table. While getting my rubdown, I was given some Hagen Das ice cream. John was there. He asked if I was hungry. My response was, of course, yes, but I also wanted to celebrate!

The next day was spent in the Jacuzzi telling Ironman stories.

At the trophy presentation that evening, we gorged ourselves on banana and coconut cream pies.

Professional triathletes who won overall were called to the stage. My "hero," Scott Allen, took second in the overall men's division. I had pasted a picture of his lean muscled legs on my garage door to inspire me during training. My "ultrahero," Dave Scott, took first place. Next, the overall woman winner received her trophy, and then each five-year age category, from the youngest to the oldest. Since I was in the oldest women's age category, mine was called last. The women who came in first, second, and third place were called on the stage. What a blast! I literally floated up to the stage. The race organizer placed beautiful leis around the necks of all three of us. We also received a medal and a plaque.

|Receiving third-place trophy for women's fifty to fifty-four age category at the Ironman trophy presentation| Dave Scott won his seventh Ironman that year in just under eight hours.

The next day my friends headed home, and I headed for Maui for a two-day rest at the Grand Hawaiian Hotel, after which, I flew to the island of Lanai for a three-day beach party with some of my sailing friends. The Pineapple Isle Yacht Club was brought back to life. I met some new friends that had their boat anchored in Lani harbor. They invited me to sail back to Oahu with them. With a gentle breeze in our sails, we headed toward Honolulu.

When I returned home, Bob brought me copies of the

newspaper and magazine articles written about the two local triathletes that participated in the race. The other person was a good friend and one of Bob's professors at Ventura College. He crewed on our boat on offshore sailboat races. We nicknamed him "gooey nuts" because he was good at slathering nuts and bolts on our boat with a rubberized compound that kept the bolts from loosening.

Newspapers and a TV station interviewed me. Guys looked me in the eye and gave me a hearty handshake, instead of a hug.

Post Race and My Mother's Death

Two weeks after the Ironman, I turned fifty-one years old. Figuring out what I was going to do next wasn't a difficult decision. I started to go on snow ski trips with the local ski club and entered several ski races. My legs were strong, and I did well.

My social life, which had been put on hold during my long hours of training, resumed. In the spring of 1986 I did a lot of sailboat racing with Bob on our twenty-seven foot Santa Cruz sailboat.

Ventura Yacht Club hosted an all-woman-crew sailboat regatta between several yacht clubs up and down the Southern California coastline. Participating yacht clubs were allowed two boats. Experienced, knowledgeable, and competitive female racers were chosen to represent each yacht club. I sailed for Pacific Corinthian Yacht Club. There were three offshore races over a two-day period. We had good wind and sunny skies.

All the male racers piled on spectator boats lining the course. They cheered and jeered us on. Our PCYC team flew the club burgee proudly off our boats backstays during the three races, not making any big mistakes; spinnaker sets were perfect, and mark roundings were crisp. We beat out the other yacht club entries and were declared the winning club. Our attractive engraved-glass sailboat trophy sits in the Ventura Yacht Club trophy case.

|*Women's Regatta crew on Zipper, a PCYC boat*|

My work as an executive secretary at Vitro, a military engineering contractor, was busy, but the job was nothing to write home about. A job change was imminent. I was heading into my eighth year as a single person. Social activities with numerous friends, sailing, skiing, biking, running on the beach, and going to work for an architect and contractor as a bookkeeper kept life rolling along.

Bob was starting to do long-distance sailboat racing on bigger boats, so I decided to sell *Saltshaker* because it was too much for me to keep the boat race-ready by myself. In retrospect, I should have hung on to the boat, because I was about to meet the love of my life and he wanted to learn how to sail.

My mom moved in with me for a short time after her husband passed away, then moved to an assisted-care facility. Outliving two husbands caused her great sadness. Her health had started to decline. She passed away from Alzheimer's disease later that year.

The last time I saw Mom alive was when she, my brother, and I sat together in the garden of the rest home where she was living. Robert and I laughed as Mom told about romping around in the barn with the Garfield kids, who lived down the road from my grandparents' farm. Her mind had returned to her childhood, and her body was wasting away. She was seventy-eight years old when she died.

Mom was buried next to my dad at Rose Hills Cemetery. I hope they are fishing together on a beautiful lake in heaven.

I say good morning to Mom and Pop when I kayak or run early in the morning. They brought joy to my life and were the kind of parents any child would be fortunate and proud to have.

Bob and I were the last of our close family. He lived down the street. We saw each other, sometimes when he was surfing on the beach and I was running in the sand, but we didn't cross paths often.

Mother's Day was not in my thought process after losing Rex and my mom. Bob called and said he had a surprise for me and to hold the day open for an adventure with him. He showed up early in the morning with a borrowed mountain bike for me. We put the bike alongside his bike in his truck and headed for Santa Paula. Topa-Topa is a rugged mountain range behind this little town. An orange orchard landscape led us to the mountain we were going to climb. I had never been on a mountain bike, only road bikes. Tires, frame, and shocks are beefier on mountain bikes, allowing the rider to ride over rough terrain without worrying about a tire blowout or a frame breaking apart. The shocks make a cushier ride over ruts and boulders. Bob and I ground up the steep mountain, sweating heavily. It was a good workout. Once on top, the view is incredible. Four offshore islands are visible: Catalina, Anacapa, Santa Cruz, and Santa Rosa. The coastline between Los Angeles and Santa Barbara lay before us. At this point, Bob brought out a Mother's Day card and a corsage from his backpack. I started to cry from heartfelt happiness. He then brought out a bottle of champagne (no glasses). We whopped it up for a bit, then hopped on our bikes for a downhill thrill I had never experienced before. Rocks and ruts were no challenge for our mountain bikes. We flew around the curves in the road, descending quickly down the mountainside. This was an uplifting day!

CHAPTER 6

A New Beginning; Marriage to Walt

John Walter Bond

The Los Padres Ski Club hosted a Christmas party. My newfound freedom from hard-core triathlon training gave me time to have a little fun. I dressed up a bit and drove to the function. While standing among a group of fellow skiers, my friend Lois came up and introduced me to a guy that liked to hike, because she knew I liked to hike. After meeting Walt Bond, we exchanged pleasantries and both moved on to chat with other people.

Lois had a private Christmas party a week later. I had been working long hours and also training for a short-distance triathlon, so I was pretty zonked. I took a nap after dinner and set the alarm for 8:00 p.m. The alarm went off. I debated if I really wanted to make the effort to go to a party. I dragged myself out of bed and got dressed, and when I arrived at the party, the first person I saw was the guy who liked to hike.

Since I was always hungry, I concentrated on the table of food. Walt drifted by and talked to me about how he wanted to learn to sail and snow ski. He seemed sincere in his quest to learn these activities, and I liked his inquisitive manner. Walt left the party early because he was going hiking early the next morning.

A few weeks later I thought about the gentle and interesting man that I talked to at the party, but I didn't know his last name or phone number. I called the ski club chairman and told him there was a guy named Walt that had joined the ski club recently, and I wanted to get his phone number. Well, I got it and placed a call. Walt wasn't home, but I left a message, including my phone number, and asked if he wanted to go hiking with me sometime. He called back after he returned home from a banjo-playing weekend in Malibu.

We set up a date to hike, but the day we picked, it was pouring rain. Walt called and said he was sorry we couldn't go. I asked him to come to my home anyway and enjoy the breakfast I had prepared for us. He said yes.

After a big scrumptious breakfast of homemade muffins, bacon, eggs, fruit, and potatoes, we drove to Pine Mountain in northeast Ventura County. It was snowing and picturesque. I was wearing running shoes. Walt gave me his extra pair of boots so I could tromp through the snow with him. They made my toes hurt but kept my feet dry. Throughout the day he was warmly sympathetic and caring about my mom's recent passing.

After bringing me home that evening, he asked me to lunch the next day. At lunch he asked me to dinner that evening. This went on for the next two days. On the third day I asked him over for dinner. My fried chicken, mashed potatoes, and gravy are killer. Everyone loves the feast. Walt played the banjo while I hopped around in the kitchen. The rest is history. We've been together ever since.

Kayaking is an activity I love. I asked Walt to join me on a harbor paddle. It was a cold winter evening. We drove over to my friend John's waterfront home. I stored two kayaks on his dock. Wearing several layers of clothing, with a wool hat pulled down over his ears, Walt carefully lowered himself into one of the kayaks. I took off in the other kayak. We paddled about one hundred yards into the dark, choppy waters. I heard a splash and turned to see Walt flailing in the water, his kayak upside down. He had a smile on his face—my kind of a guy!

Walt hung onto my boat, and I pulled the kayak and him back to the dock. We gathered up all the wet clothes, went back to my condo and jumped in the hot Jacuzzi. The two of us had grown to love each other and were inseparable. Two weeks later we knew we wanted to marry one another.

On one of these special evenings, Bob came by to hang a new front door for me. I introduced Bob to Walt, and we told him we were going to get married. This caused a warm and friendly conversation, while I fixed dinner. Walt helped Bob hang the door. Bob could see how much in love we were and was happy that I had found someone so special.

We set a date to get married a year away. Walt was just coming out of a divorce.

This man of many attributes is truly a renaissance man. Walt has no ego, is self-confident, and shows vulnerability, without trying to cover it up. He is brilliant (his IQ places him in the top 1 percent of the nation), honest, and totally committed to his obligations. He also plays ballads on the guitar, sings, and plays knee-slappin' tunes on the banjo. Walt is extremely well read and educated, with a master's degree in mathematics from UC Riverside and a master's degree and PhD in computer science from UCLA. Walt is a well-built man with radiant blue eyes. He was forty-one when I met him. I was fifty-two.

Walt moved into my Channel Islands Harbor condo. Many evenings after work we walked across the street to the beach and sat on the sand, watching the sunset. We both had personal issues we needed to vent.

Walt's previous marriage had been an unhappy one. His wife

was rigid, unyielding, and contemptuous to Walt. He had two children with her, who also treated him badly. They were young adults when Walt filed for divorce. Walt's anger had built up to the point where he knew the negatives far outweighed the positives, and marriage was no longer possible. I sat beside him in the sand, held his hand, and listened to him.

I was holding in grief from Rex's death that I had never had the courage to face. I had not been strong enough to purge my emotions by myself. Walt held me close as we sat on the beach; my body shook with tears and sobs.

Two tall, statuesque trees stand on a hill in Ventura. They are visible while driving up the coast from Channel Islands Harbor to Ventura. I had always thought these two trees symbolized my strong and resolute sons. Since Rex's death, it had become unendurable for me to look at the trees. Walt thought going up on the hill where the trees stood might be a healing process for my grief.

We hiked up to the bluff where the two trees stood. Walt asked me to touch them both. It was difficult. The experience helped me to understand that my love for both my sons stands tall, never to be diminished, in both life and death.

I also understood that grief over Rex's death would never go away, but I felt I had the strength to tolerate the loss and not pine over what Rex could have become, but rather, who he was and how fortunate I had been to be his mom and friend.

Marriage to Walt

Walt's and my courtship was short. We saw no reason to delay getting married. Neither of us had reservations about spending the rest of our lives together. I lack the formal education Walt has attained; however, we share the same values and standards.

Since our marriage, life for me has been an enlightened educational process because of my husband's magnanimous influence.

There have been many times when each other's behavior changed because it made common sense, and we wish to be respectful and considerate. Neither of us tries to change the other. I'm a neat-neck, and Walt doesn't see mess. He has become neater, and I have a more relaxed attitude about having books and shoes left where they were put down. We continue to grow.

One of Walt's goals when I met him was the completion of the BMTC (basic mountaineering training course) through the Sierra Club. I asked him if I could join him in this endeavor. The hiking I had done with ski club buddies was unstructured and pretty wild. My hiking backpack included charcoal, a piece of meat, lighter fluid, and a sleeping bag. I had never heard of the ten essentials—extra clothing, food and water, matches, first-aid kit, tent, rain gear, compass, map, and sunscreen. Walt adds an eleventh essential—a twenty-dollar bill.

A conditioning hike was my first BMTC adventure. The hike was in the San Bernardino Mountains, with a three-thousand-foot elevation gain over seventeen miles. I was in better shape than most of the hikers. After reaching the summit, the downhill phase was fun. I was feeling frisky. Some of the hikers were getting low on water. I volunteered to run down to the car at the bottom of the trail and fetch more water for them. This action was nothing for me, and the hikers appreciated getting their thirst quenched.

On the rock climbing and compass trail map instruction weekend, Walt and I enjoyed the overnight outing: hiking through the desert and pinpointing our course on a trail map, climbing rocks with ropes lifting us to the top of rock faces, and then belaying ourselves back down. We also spent lots of time in our tent. At the next BMTC meeting, we were awarded the "lip-locking award" for the outing.

Ice-ax practice occurred on a weekend outing in the high

Sierras. We parked our car in a couple of feet of snow and donned snowshoes. We had our tent, sleeping bags, food, ten essentials, and Svea stoves in our backpacks. After setting up camp in a snow-covered forest, Walt and I thought it might be fun to fly a kite. He fell into a stream while walking backward with the kite string. He had six inches of ice on the bottom of his snowshoes when he finally pulled himself out of the icy water. We had no fire to warm him—snuggling together in the tent worked just fine.

There were several hikes into the mountains of Riverside County. Eventually, we became impatient with the dogma associated with structured camping and never completed the BMTC program. I think I was a bad influence. We lost all contact with the Sierra Club.

I knew of a unique restaurant in Ojai. It was where my friend John had taken me after my disastrous marathon in San Diego. I asked Walt for a date. We drove into the mountains above Ojai where the restaurant was located. There are hot spring tubs in the building behind the restaurant. We entered one of the closed-off hot tub rooms. After a half hour of jumping from the hot tub into an adjacent cold tub, a small bell rang above the door and an attendant announced that our massage room was ready. We put on robes that were laid out for us. A joint massage awaited us. Walt and I held hands while our bodies were being stroked. After this procedure we were in ecstasy. We managed to put our clothes on and sauntered down a gravel path that led us to an elegant five-star restaurant. We had an exquisite gourmet meal. On the way home, somehow, our car took us into the middle of an orange grove. We were lost but didn't care.

Sailing was a big part of my life, and I wanted to share my passion for ocean sailing with Walt. We rented a sailboat from a Channel Islands boat club and sailed off toward Santa Cruz Island. The weather was warm and pleasant. A five-hour sail took us to the back side of the island. We anchored in Cochise Inlet, cracked a beer, and sat in the cockpit to enjoy the view and launch our rubber dinghy. It was late afternoon when we rode our raft to shore. The hills behind us had a hiking trail that wound its way up to a cliff that overlooked our anchorage and Albert's Anchorage, just east of us. After hiking the trail, we stood on top of the cliff and watched the two boats that had been in our anchorage take off. We were alone. It seemed natural to play Adam and Eve for the rest of our visit to this pristine paradise. There were warm pools of water trapped by low tide on the beach. This was our spa. Walt was hooked. He loved sailing.

Walt had spent many summers in the mountains of Colorado and New Mexico while growing up. His wedding gift to me was sharing his knowledge of these areas. We poured over maps of the southwestern United States to plan our honeymoon. A route was decided upon and laid out, within the constraints of a two-week vacation.

On May 21, 1987, we jumped in our little Honda Hatchback car packed with camping gear, guitar and banjo, and a tandem bicycle on top. We drove by to say good-bye to my boss, who was overseeing the renovation of a nearby beach house. I had already told him, "I'm off to marry Walt, and he is my priority, so I am quitting work."

Being an employee of the son of an ex-boyfriend had had its benefits. My boss was always extra nice and respectful to me. His dad, John Sr., is a highly successful businessman, an ex-Marine, and airline pilot. When Walt and I became serious about getting married, I went to John's office building, closed his office door, and told him I had fallen in love with a guy I had recently met. I also told him I couldn't go to Australia with him. (Bob had flown to Australia to outfit a seventy-two-foot sloop, to be sailed from Australia to the United States. John and I were to do the Australia to New Zealand leg with Bob across the Tasman Sea.) After telling my story, I watched John's jaw drop. However, being the terrific gentleman he is, John said he was happy for me and looked forward to being introduced to Walt. After meeting each other, they have become good friends. The three of us have had some enjoyable sailing and kayaking outings together.

Walt and I were embarking on a new life. The pragmatic method of beginning our honeymoon was to get married somewhere along the way. Las Vegas, Nevada was a quick solution. The marriage license bureau issued our license. I was so excited I couldn't remember my mother's middle name, which is required on the form. It came to me after taking a deep breath.

We walked across the street and were married by a justice of the peace (old crotchety guy who was sitting on the steps of the county courthouse with his buddy—both sharing a bottle of booze hidden inside of the paper bag they passed between them). They took us to a very small room on an upper floor of the Las Vegas Courthouse and closed the door. The guy who was designated as justice of the peace asked if we had wedding rings to place on his little velvet pad. We answered no. Walt and I did not wear rings and thought them frivolous in the commitment of marriage. Also, jewelry is in opposition to the essence of goin' to weather, which entails not burdening yourself with useless adornment.

The old, disreputable-looking justice of the peace put the pad back in the drawer of the desk, the only furniture in the room. We stood before him wearing our running shorts and matching Valentine's Day "Sweetheart Run" T-shirts we had received in a 10k run in Santa Barbara a couple of months before. The justice read from the Good Book while his buddy looked on, witnessing our ceremony.

Walt and I exchanged vows. We kissed, hugged each other and the two derelict justices, and gave the guy with the Bible twenty dollars. To record this extremely momentous occasion, the justice took a mug shot of us with our camera, as we stood against the blank baby-shit-yellow wall of the little room.

We flew down the steps of the old courthouse, not spending

one more second on the wedding thing, and took off in the car to begin the all-important honeymoon!

There is a beautiful canyon between Las Vegas and St. George, Utah. While driving through this area, Walt serenaded me with the folk song "Cotton Jenny—The Wheels of Love Go Round." We thought we were the luckiest people alive.

That evening we pitched our tent in among the magnificent buttes of Zion National Park. Happiness was an understatement, as we continued on the next day to the North Rim of the Grand Canyon. Lush forests, majestic canyons and secluded hiking trails made this area another romantic camping spot.

We continued on to the small town of Delores, near the four corners area of Colorado, New Mexico, Arizona, and Utah. This is where the Colorado Mountains begin their climb up and over Lizard Head Pass and into the ski resort of Telluride.

A local market in Delores sold us groceries for our dinner and breakfast the next morning. We looked up at the mountains where we were headed. Dark thunderheads had formed, and it looked like a storm was brewing. We forged on with our plan to camp by the Delores River for the night.

The climb on the road out of town was steep and twisted around huge boulders and aspen trees. Walt spotted a river crossing. We turned off and followed a little dirt road to a small camp site along the river, with a picnic table and fire pit. We were back in the woods, all alone.

After setting up our tent next to the river, Walt built a fire so we could cook dinner. Inclement weather stayed at bay while we set up camp and ate. With our stomachs full, we sat by the fire drinking an after-dinner rum and hot chocolate. The sky opened up. We dove into our tent and finished our drinks, while listening to the rain and thunder. The next morning we peered outside. The rain had turned to snow during the night. The sun was coming up, and we spotted a doe and her faun grazing in the snow-dusted meadow across the river. The air was chilly. Walt built a fire to warm us and to heat the coffee pot and breakfast grill. No six-star hotel could even come close to our radiant experience.

|Honeymoon campsite on the Delores River in southwest Colorado|

Walt pointed our little Honda eastward toward the Collegiate Mountains, on the eastern side of the Colorado Rockies. The mountains in this spectacular range are all over fourteen thousand feet. We stood on the bank of the Taylor River, looking up to see snow-capped mountains off in the distance.

The Taylor River runs below Cottonwood Pass, south of Crested Butte, where I had skied during my single life. This area is a beautiful summertime mountain bike, fishing, and hiking playground. We rented a cabin so we could take a shower and dry the tent out. The cabin was just a few feet from the river bank. Walt caught several trout and cleaned them, and I cooked the fish for dinner.

More exploration of the Rocky Mountains had to wait. We headed southwest, out of the mountains, and drove to the South Rim of the Grand Canyon. We hiked and biked around the rim and had our last campfire.

Our two-week honeymoon was over. Walt and I had begun what was to become a lifelong honeymoon.

Sally Bond

East Coast Fun

For me, the eastern half of the United States was unexplored territory. Walt went back to the Aerospace Corporation to work. They gave him five weeks vacation a year. It didn't take us long to embark on our next trip.

We flew to New York, stayed in Queens, took a subway to downtown, and walked forty-seven blocks through iconic boulevards where the Twin Towers stood above the National Cathedral. Taking photos of the city from on top of the Empire State Building was enthralling. We caught a ferry ride to the Statue of Liberty. New York, New York—I loved the city.

Walt played tour guide in Boston, where he went to high school. We took a low-flying biplane out over Cape Cod. The sun shone brightly on beach cottages and pleasure boats tied up on wooden wharfs.

Small-masted boats were anchored in inlets as we drove through Maine. Their hardy sailors are prepared for the full force of Mother Nature. A work boat carried us to an offshore island for an overnight stay. We rented a cabin that was perched out over the water. The island's only restaurant was next door. Customers sat at rickety card tables. Walt devoured a two-pound lobster for dinner. I ran around the island the next morning and watched fishermen ready their nets and lobster traps for the day's work that lay ahead.

We stood on a deserted beach on Cape Breton Island, where the English explorer John Cabot landed his ship *The Matthew* in 1497. A strong sea breeze swept sand into our faces. I hung onto Walt so I wouldn't blow away.

A ferryboat took us across the windy Northumberland Strait to Prince Edward Island. It was a bumpy, wet ride. We drove our car off the ferry and found the island sparsely populated. A sign by the road directed us to a farmhouse B&B. It was perfect—we had a friendly host and a cozy bedroom where we spent the night. A hike down a rutted trail the next morning brought us to a towering red-and-white-striped lighthouse building. Walt and I climbed circular steps that led to the illuminated lighthouse beacon, signaling ships at sea to navigate around the rocky shoreline. We spotted huge waves offshore. Our ferry ride back to the mainland meant crashing into heavy seas.

Quebec City blew my socks off. It is the oldest European settlement and oldest fort north of Mexico. Quebec was the headquarters of raids against New England during the French and Indian Wars in the early 1760s. One could feel the history of this beautiful city. The restaurant where we ate lunch had twelve-foot-thick brick walls. French cuisine served by French-speaking waiters added to our unique experience. Cannons line the city's coastal positions, a leftover remembrance of the war years.

We headed south through New York state on our way to LaGuardia Airport, stopping at picturesque Lake Champlain. A decisive battle in the War of 1812 was fought here, which ended the British invasion of our northern states and denied the British control of the Great Lakes region. A war scene was hard to fathom in the peaceful landscape of pleasure boats anchored in front of lovely homes overlooking the lake. Leaves were turning red and golden across endless foothills and waterways on our drive south. The beauty of the East Coast surprised me.

There was more East Coast exploring on our docket. Walt had a seminar in Chicago the following summer. We packed an extra suitcase full of camping gear and flew to the "Windy City." After the seminar ended, we hit the road in a small convertible and headed north through the Wisconsin Dells, camping at state parks along the way.

Our focus was to explore Michigan. We reached the southern shore of Lake Superior, where the Apostle Islands jut out into the lake. Beautiful weather allowed us to explore the islands by boat and dry out our mud-soaked tent on the B&B verandah where we holed up for a couple of nights.

Driving east through Lake of the Clouds was delightful. Rich forests surround the lake. We hiked along trails that wound through a golden canopy of mammoth trees. The leaves were turning into brilliant fall colors.

The highway follows the lake shoreline. A slim finger of land juts out into the middle of Lake Superior. The city of Hancock is about halfway up the finger. This small college town is Walt's birthplace. Folks that live here call themselves Uppers, a designation of living in uppermost Michigan—rugged country where robust people devour pasties (meat pies), and the weather is cold and nasty. The peninsula ends at Copper Harbor, the terminus for ferry rides to Isle Royal National Park, located in the remote reaches of Lake Superior.

Onward to Sault Ste. Marie. Lady luck shined on us. A ferryboat was about to leave for Mackinaw Island, a unique resort off the northern coast of Lake Michigan. We grabbed our toothbrushes and hopped aboard the ferry. Their tourist bureau provided us with a reservation at a Mackinaw Island harbor-view B&B with a fireplace and Jacuzzi. Another idyllic evening was about to begin.

The next morning we hiked through a park in the middle of the island to the Grand Hotel, where Christopher Reeve starred in a film called *Somewhere in Time*. Everything about this hotel is grand. The wood exterior is painted brilliant white. Gables and porches exude an imposing facade. Interior furnishings are luxurious. Velvet cushions and long tassels on the drapes give the hotel a bygone-era appearance. I had time to run clear around the small island before a big rainstorm hit. Transportation on Mackinaw is limited to horse-drawn carts. Restaurants serve roasted garlic, steak, and all the trimmings. I can still conjure up the taste and smell of the roasted garlic Walt and I smeared on some fresh baked bread.

Before boarding the ferry that took us back to the mainland, I bought a terrific Mackinaw Island Yacht Race sweatshirt. Bob had raced in this prestigious race a couple of years prior. The sailboat race begins in Chicago and races to and from Mackinaw Island, with an overnight stop on the island.

We headed south to Dearborn to tour the Henry Ford Museum. The extensive museum displays innovative inventions from the past and present. We were particularly taken with the replica of a bike shop where the Wright Brothers designed the airplane they flew at Kitty Hawk.

We had circumnavigated Lake Michigan and got our feet wet in Lake Superior. The area is full of tough-minded and hard-working people. I liked their attitude.

Saline Valley

A brand-new stripped-out Toyota van became our versatile camping vehicle, after a redesign to accommodate large boxes in the shape of coffins behind the two front seats, making a wall to wall platform to sleep on. The lids had padded carpeting on top. These boxes held our camping gear, clothes, and food.

Saline Valley is a few miles south of Death Valley. We drove from Channel Islands Harbor north to Barstow and headed onto a dirt road that took us deep into Saline Valley. Our tinny van almost fell apart on the washboard road, but boy, was this worth the drive. High mountain ranges ring the valley. The infamous Saline Hot Springs awaited us. After looking around the campsite, it became obvious that this was a nudist happening. Everyone was nonchalantly bare-ass naked. Walt and I thought this was cool. We stripped and jumped into the nearest hot spring tub. A very dignified couple from New York sat on the rocky edge of the pool with a bottle of champagne and some liver pâté. We found that all pretentious talk falls by the wayside when there is nothing to hide. Enjoyable and interesting conversation came easily, even though we were strangers. The stars blazed overhead that night. We woke up several times during the night to crawl out of our sleeping bags to sit in a hot tub, mesmerized by stargazing.

Our little retreat ended too soon. It was time to get back home and into the swing of things, listen to the news, and see what was happening outside our little world.

Peaceful Times

Clinging to Reagan's coattails, George H. W. Bush was elected forty-first president in 1988 on the Republican ticket. He was a sincere and ethical president.

In December 1991, the USSR was dissolved, and the independence of non-Russian republics was recognized.

Most of these republics were unfamiliar to me because of my lack of knowledge in foreign geography and history. Since I was now free from having to hold a job down, there was time to read and listen to news reports regarding international issues. Also, in 1991 the Internet was made available to unrestricted use. The number of host computers reached one million. Walt and I were among those million. I learned that a computer can expand horizons and be a vehicle to limitless knowledge.

Bush was not an exciting, or charismatic president, but he was a well-respected foreign policy leader. In his book *Second Chance*. Zbigniew Brzezinski, national security adviser to President Carter, stated: "Bush focused primarily on the delicate task of peacefully managing the dismantling of the Soviet empire and then on cutting Saddam Hussein's excessive ambitions down to size."

On his second run as a presidential candidate, Bush was out of touch with most Americans because he isolated himself in the elite atmosphere of the rich and powerful. He had no idea what a loaf of bread or a gallon of gas cost. The no-drama president was about to be sidelined.

Bill Clinton won the 1992 presidential election on the Democratic ticket. He was a political unknown from Hope, Arkansas, where he was a one-term governor. Clinton was a young president who brought energy and new ideas to the White House.

In one of his first moves as president, Clinton established the controversial "don't ask, don't tell" policy for homosexuals in the military. There was a big ruckus in Washington, predominantly among the religious-right Republicans, who proclaimed that it was a sin to be gay and that our military troops should not have to serve in the same military that enlisted and tolerated gays.

The president delegated his wife, Hillary, to head a commission to overhaul health care, by giving all Americans universal health-care coverage—a one-payer system. Health insurance companies went ballistic. The plan proved to be too radical and did not gain sufficient support. Many people were without health care, and more and more employees were losing health-care benefits from their employer. Medical costs were growing at an astronomical rate because cost containment was not being addressed.

NAFTA (North American Free Trade Agreement) took effect in January 1994. Ross Perot ran for president in 1992 on the Independent ticket, touting the negatives of this agreement, by saying that American jobs would be lost, and we would hear a giant sucking sound of these jobs being filled by cheap labor in other countries.

His insightful prescience came home to roost. America has lost millions of jobs to Mexican, South American, and Asian cheap labor. Our manufacturing base dwindled. US manufacturing companies moved their plants abroad to take advantage of lower tax rates, less regulation, and low worker costs.

The Clinton administration lasted eight years. More on how both Bill and Hillary entertained us later.

Hawaii Camping Trip

Walt had not been to Hawaii. It was time for me to play tour guide. We did the extra suitcase containing our camping gear routine and flew to Maui. Instead of heading east out of the airport where multitudes of hotels and condos line the shoreline, we drove west toward the less populated and lush road to Hana, passing numerous waterfalls, beautiful sandy beaches, and a rusted-out Volkswagen sitting on the side of the road. Wild flowers engulfed the dilapidated old car. Seven Pools Campground is beyond Hana and sits in a grassy meadow, overlooking the ocean. Plummeting water travels down the mountainside, spilling from one pool into the next. Grottos ring the pools. We jumped out of the car and climbed up the falls, perching ourselves on rocks, letting water fall over our bodies.

We pitched our tent on the verdant campsite lawn and set up an ocean view outdoor kitchen. This was the noncommercial Hawaii that I promised Walt. Early the next morning I went on a run down a nearby deserted road. It started to rain, so I made a turn down another road that had an umbrella of banyan trees lining the road. Off to the left I spotted a small church and ran up to it and a grave yard that overlooked the ocean. One grave was heavily decorated with flowering plants. I stopped and took a deep breath. This was grave site of Charles Lindbergh, the first person to fly solo from the United States to Europe. I ran back to our campsite and commandeered Walt to come see what I found. It had stopped raining. We stood, remembering the man whose life's successes and tragedies dominated the news for years.

After a few days of frolicking in sheltered pools and grottos, Walt was covered with mosquito bites. It was time to pack up our goods and head for the Maui airport for a flight to Kauai. A woman behind us commented on Walt's measles-like legs when we climbed the ramp into the airplane.

A state park is on top of Kauai's Na Pali coastline cliffs. We stayed in one of their cabins and hiked the trails along the rim. The view encapsulates steep cliffs covered with copious foliage, endless ocean, white-sand beaches far below, and cascading waterfalls. We were the only ones staying in the park. Our cabin cost seven dollars a night and slept six people.

Another Na Pali state park sits at ocean level. Access is through the funky town of Hanalei. The road ends where the Na Pali coastline begins, at Haena State Park. We placed our tent in beach sand. The front flapper of our tent opened up to a view of ocean waves, just yards away. The Na Pali coastline was the view out the back window of our tent. Farther down on the beach a group of Hawaiians were grilling some fish they had caught. One of them walked over and invited us to join their feast. We grabbed some brews and headed to where the party was. Ukulele music and song lasted long after the stars popped out.

There were no clouds on top of the cliffs early the next morning. We quickly put on our hiking boots and headed for the rocky trail along the Na Pali coastline that leads to, as I remembered, the most beautiful beach I had ever seen. When we reached this paradise, we ditched our boots and ran through the surf, sat in the sand, and took in the view. Turning away from the ocean, we started a lengthy hike through dense jungle to Hanakapiai Falls. The path was muddy and hard to follow. Finally, we spotted a colossal waterfall through the treetops. We were almost there. The large pool of water around the falls was cold. We jumped in and jumped out quickly.

On the hike back out to the beach, all I could think of was tropical tacos. We were both hungry. Luck was with us; the guy who made the tacos still had his little trailer sitting next to the Hanalei River. Just as I had sat with Bob, my ex-husband Bill, and our friends after hiking the Na Pali coastline, my husband Walt and I sat along the riverbank enjoying a tropical taco and a cold one.

We spotted some kayakers paddling on the river. This seemed like a hot idea. The kayak rental place was not far away. Once we settled into our kayaks, we paddled softly through canals where flowers and lush ferns line the banks of the river. The water spilled out into the ocean. We were now kayaking in Hanalei Bay. Boy, did this bring back memories. There weren't many boats in the anchorage, which allowed us to explore the sea life beneath us and look up at the mountains behind us. This was a superb way to continue our quest for an endless blissful marriage.

Cabo Boat Delivery

Travel was becoming more than a pastime; it became a way of life. Our eyes and ears were always open to new adventures.

Bob was hired to race a sixty-six-foot Peterson racing sloop from Los Angeles Harbor to Cabo San Lucas, Mexico. His contract included delivering the boat back to LA after the race. Al was part of the racing crew and boat delivery team. Walt and I rounded out the crew to sail from Mexico to California—we flew to Cabo.

Our duffel bags in hand, we took a taxi from the airport to where the Peterson was tied up in the harbor. Bob welcomed us aboard and showed us our bunks. After drinking a beer with the racing crew and finding out the scuttlebutt between rival boats, we all took off for the trophy presentation being held at a luxurious hotel on the Pacific side of Cabo. Margarita bars, mariachi bands, and well-oiled sailors brought a lively mix to the scene. I spotted Rambo (Sylvester Stalone) at a margarita fountain. Walt and I were getting tipsy off the atmosphere. We asked Bob if we could use his room at the hotel for a bit. He snickered and threw the room key to Walt. Tequila makes some people crazy. The surf was just beyond the hotel and across a sandy beach. Jumping into the ocean nude was where we were headed. We ran out the door, hand in hand. Unbeknownst to us, floodlight from the hotel roof lit our way. Loud applause greeted us. We'd been spotted by the party animals. Walt and I crouched down and crawled back to the hotel room, put on our clothes, ran out the door, and headed for the surf. Once we descended down a berm, the hotel lights were in shadow. We dumped our clothes and ran into the surf. What fun; however, when we exited the water all we could see were bright lights. We had a heck of a time finding our clothes. After taking a shower, it occurred to us we were hungry, so we tracked Bob down and gave him back the hotel room key. Walt and I flagged a taxi to take us to a restaurant that served lobster. Now nourished with a big dinner, we hiked back to the harbor. There were lights from a restaurant on the cliff above where our boat was moored. A cup of coffee sounded good, so we started crawling up the hillside to the restaurant. We fell into sewer water flowing down the hill and into the harbor, so had to say uncle. The next challenge was getting aboard the boat, which was tied up to several other large race boats by dock lines. I reached up and hand-over-handed my body up onto the first boat. Walt fell into the water. We finally wrestled our way onto the Peterson. Walt was grimy with brown, yucky stuff from head to toe. He took his soaked wallet out of his pocket and gingerly laid out his driver's license, credit cards, and other precious items on the chart table. We tumbled into bed.

Bob woke us up the next morning to tell us he was going marlin fishing. We both needed more recuperation from our previous night's escapades. It was back to our bunk and more rest, instead of going marlin fishing with Bob and his mates.

After clearing customs the following day, we motor-sailed out of the harbor and headed up the coast. It was breezy but sunny and warm. It was my turn at the helm. I stood barefooted on top of the cockpit seats to see over the bow while steering the boat. I had a headset on, listening to Divo. The coast was lined with rugged mountains. Bob, Walt, and Al were lazed out on the deck. Seagulls soared over our heads.

Racing sailboats don't have large gas tanks. We headed for Turtle Bay to get a fill-up. It was Thanksgiving. Before leaving home, I had packed an extra bag with a canned ham, sweet potatoes, canned pumpkin, a pie shell, and all the fixings for a holiday dinner. This was a break in our diet from eating the marlin Bob had caught in Cabo.

Night sailing can be rapturous, if the weather cooperates. We didn't experience any severe wind or waves. Stars reach the horizon in all directions; the sky and water are black and indistinguishable. Trusting the compass is paramount. Walt was becoming a full-fledged sailor and enjoying the camaraderie of offshore sailing with our small crew.

Mazatlan Boat Delivery

Early the next spring, another boat delivery opportunity surfaced. Bob was racing a fifty-foot Bill Lee ultralight to Mazatlan and asked Walt and me to be part of the delivery crew from there back to LA. At the last minute, Walt had a work commitment in Colorado Springs. Bob's crew was his wife, Gail, sailing buddy, Matt, and myself. Gail and I flew to Mazatlan. I missed Walt. While provisioning the boat for the long haul up the coast, Bob bought a toy telephone for me to call Walt on. He and the rest of the crew were tired of hearing me lament the fact I didn't have my hubby with me. This was before shipboard communications allowed phone calls, and before cell-phone technology.

The sail between Mazatlan and Cabo was pristine. Warm breezes and sunny skies lasted until we turned north up the coast. Fierce winds and heavy seas had us bundled up in foul-weather gear. The wind worsened, day by day. We had a bladder full of diesel fuel on the cockpit floor. Wave action caused it to spring a leak. We were tracking the slippery mess down below deck. It was necessary to seek refuge to clean up the diesel. Luckily, there was an offshore island ahead. We were able to anchor off the lee of the island long enough to fill the gas tank with what was left in the bladder and wash the rest of the residue away. It was late afternoon when we pulled back out to sea. I kept looking at the wind-velocity meter. It registered thirty-eight knots and climbed to forty-three knots. We were in for another rough night. Matt and I were on the one to three watch. The ocean looked menacing. It was pitch black. We spotted a gigantic wave off our beam, heading right for us. We had to tack on the wave to avoid being dismasted. The boat lifted, and then crashed down on the back side of the rogue wave. The shackle holding the running backstay exploded. Bob was jarred from his sleep and knew all hell was breaking loose on deck. He tore out of his bunk and gave us a hand. The shackle was replaced; we did not dismast, and we could safely tack the boat again.

By the time we reached San Diego to clear customs, we were tired, weather-worn, and had lost a few pounds on our journey because it had been impossible to cook during our rough voyage. I found a real phone and called Walt. He had returned from his business trip and immediately jumped in the car and drove from his work site in El Segundo to San Diego. Bob, Gail, Matt, and I went to a restaurant for breakfast. We must have been a forlorn sight. Our clothes were soaking wet, and our eyes were bright red from salt spray. Walt was standing on the dock beside our boat when we returned from breakfast. Welcoming hugs lasted a long time.

Seek Fulfillment

In between sailing adventures, life in Channel Islands Harbor was all about kayaking, running on the beach, and socializing. However, driving sixty miles along the Pacific Coast Highway between home and work in El Segundo became stressful to Walt, so we decided to rent out our home and move south. We bought a great condo right across the street from the ocean in Redondo Beach, within ten miles of Walt's company. The downside was that we were not used to being in the midst of so many people. We felt this was a temporary home.

I volunteered time to a health-care counseling program that listened to the elderly who were indigent and frustrated by their lack of ability to cope with life. Sitting with people who live alone (most had severe health problems) for an hour or so, listening to them talk about their troubles, was all I was qualified to do, and was all these disenfranchised seniors wanted. Keeping them company for a small amount of time in their monotonous day was important. Serious problems were addressed by certified counselors.

I found that motivating people was difficult. Their will to lead productive lives had been destroyed. Most did not understand the process and importance of even mild exercise. Thought-provoking dialogue wasn't happening. The experience was demoralizing and depressing. We have the freedom to choose our own attitude—be curious and find purpose. It is important to try and have a life of well-being.

Dr. Viktor Frankl, who was one of Europe's leading psychoanalysts, wrote *Man's Search for Meaning*. The first part of his book details his life as a prisoner in a Nazi death camp. Frankl showed that prisoners, stripped of everything they possessed, could still hold their heads high, because their ideals were firmly implanted in their naked and tormented souls, stating, "One should not search for an abstract meaning of life. Everyone has his own specific mission to carry out a concrete assignment which demands fulfillment."

What you do during the day counts when goals are in line with values. The richness of life is boundless when we stick to, and don't deviate from, ethical standards. It has been a tough journey for me to learn how important the pursuance of worthwhile goals are to a person's fulfillment, success, and happiness throughout life.

The Art of Happiness, by Dalai Lama:

> Love and kindness cannot be regarded as a luxury. Even without religion we can manage, but without these, it is difficult to find happiness and tranquility. Much depends on the eradication of narrow-mindedness and self-centered thinking and action. With proper education, love, and kindness we can develop a sense of universal responsibility.

Gaining recognition for accomplishments is not a worthy goal. I don't know anyone who does not enjoy being recognized for an achievement; however, the achievement is primary. An unshakable sense of purpose and an immutable code of ethics should guide us.

The race is always to make yourself strong, healthy, intelligent, wise, ethical, and accomplished. Age and ability does not preclude anyone from contributing to society and self-worthiness. Having the will to try and better oneself is paramount.

There are significant lifetime achievements that, hopefully, occur within everyone's time on earth. Walt had a big one before he met me, obtaining his PhD from UCLA in computer science. I had one before I met him, placing third in my age category at the Hawaii World Championship Ironman Triathlon. Bob had a significant achievement by placing first in the Single-Handed Trans-Pac sailboat race.

In a couple of years, all three of us would rebuild a thirty-foot racing sailboat and successfully race the boat off the Channel Islands and Ventura coastline—another significant lifetime achievement.

These achievements have entailed a lot of hard work and have brought happiness and, yes, a little pride also.

Abraham Maslow, the US psychologist and philosopher best known for his self-actualization theory, wrote *Toward a Psychology of Being*. In it he said:

> Each person has a hierarchy of needs that must be satisfied, ranging from basic physiological requirements, to love, esteem, and finally, self actualization. As each need is satisfied, the next higher level in the emotional hierarchy dominates conscious functioning; thus, people who need food or shelter, or are not in a safe environment, are unable to express higher needs when survival is critical.

Most of the friends who live around us are educated and successful people. They work hard to achieve their goals: have families they can be proud of and give of themselves at the drop of a hat. They prize their station in life and protect themselves from losing what they have gained by being circumspect when making decisions. Walt and I revel in watching their children grow from childhood into adulthood, maintaining an open line of communication with them. A special treat happens on Sunday mornings. The little kids in our neighborhood come to our house and help me make french toast by cracking the eggs (picking the shells out of the bowl), stirring the eggs with gusto, and putting a secret sauce on top of the toast. Walt is the syrup mister.

Happiness, self-actualization, and achievement are not related to wealth and are not even dependent on physical wellness. A happy person is likely to be married, have many friends, and have a spiritual orientation in his or her life. Well-being is found in disciplined lifestyles, committed relationships, being self-confident, and having a willingness to give of yourself and to be compassionate, with honest intentions. Achievement is a completed hard-earned worthwhile goal.

CHAPTER 7

Vulnerabilities; Zest for Life; Boat Building; Kayaking

Angioplasty

For exercise, Walt and I ran along the Redondo Beach oceanfront boardwalk in the evening. I started having a hard time keeping up with him. I usually ran faster than him. My throat and left arm hurt. It did not occur to me there was anything wrong with my heart, since I ate a healthy diet, weighed a lean 110 pounds, had a muscular body, and was an athlete.

We were planning a hike up the highest mountain in Southern California—San Gorgonio, in the San Bernardino Mountains. This is a strenuous hike. Walt thought it prudent for me to go to a doctor and get a checkup before we did our hike. I agreed, if he wore moleskin on his ankles so he wouldn't get blisters on his feet during the hike.

The internist took one look at me and went next door and got a cardiologist. The two doctors put me on the treadmill, and I started to run. They quickly pulled me off. The cardiologist gave me nitroglycerin and told me not to move. He said my face was ashen, and I was in need of immediate surgery.

The next morning I had an angioplasty in South Bay Hospital. One of my main pumping arteries was completely closed. One collateral artery was sustaining me. After the angioplasty procedure, I was in intensive care for three days and had a slow recovery. I bounced back to health after completing rehab.

Park City Skiing Disaster

We put our South Bay condo up for sale and moved back to Channel Islands Harbor because we were about to become involved in a sailing enterprise, and we missed our life in Ventura County (nothing like a life-threatening scare to get your priorities back to basics). We were moving to where we were most comfortable.

In the winter of 1992, Walt and I went skiing in Park City, Utah, where some of our skiing friends live. The trip was over New Year's. Lots of parties were planned.

The first day out we were having a fun time skiing. While skiing down a hill late in the day Walt suddenly sat down in the snow. We looked up at him from below and saw another skier stop and plant his skies in a crossed position—a sign of needing help. We rode the lift up the hill and skied down to where Walt was sitting in the snow. He had broken his right leg, just below the knee. The ski patrol took him down the slope in a basket. An initial examination by a medical team confirmed our worst fears. Walt was taken by ambulance to the Salt Lake City Hospital. Immediate surgery was required. Bone splinters had to be removed from the tibia. The leg swelled so much before surgery that it exploded from the knee down to the ankle and turned black. It was a terrible mess to look at. I was worried. In a six hour long surgery an orthopedic surgeon removed the splinters and inserted a plate and several screws into the leg to hold the bone together. He said that Walt was lucky that the leg didn't have to be amputated. After a couple of blood transfusions and a week of recovery in the hospital, the next problem was getting him home to California on the airplane.

Our friend John wanted to fly his turboprop up to Salt Lake with Bob to bring us home. A large winter storm off the Pacific Coast precluded them from taking off.

None of the major airline carriers wanted to take Walt. They told me he needed a medevac flight from Salt Lake to LAX, which cost a fortune. His medical insurance would not cover the trip.

In desperation, I made reservations on United Airlines and did not tell the agent what kind of shape Walt was in, only that he needed a wheelchair and an aisle seat on the airplane.

After getting Walt on the airplane, I packed ice around his leg and padded it with blankets. This was not a happy time for my wonderful husband. Bob and Gail met us at LAX. It was pouring rain. We laid Walt out in the back of Bob's van and were relieved that we had him back in Southern California and almost home. Therapy, walking on crutches, and months of recuperation followed.

Boat Project

When Walt traveled to Colorado for a work-related assignment, I sometimes flew there with him so we could travel into the mountains for the weekend. On one such weekend we visited Monarch Pass, which is high in the Rockies. After a day of playing in the snow, we called Bob to tell him about our adventure. He told us he had found a thirty-foot Olsen ultralight sailboat that fit the description of the type of boat the three of us had been looking for. We told him it was a go! To celebrate, Walt and I jumped into the mountain resort Jacuzzi. It was snowing heavily. We laughed at each other's "snow cap" and dreamed about what lay before us.

By the time we returned home, Bob had taken all the hardware off the boat and was replacing it with lighter high-tech hardware. Walt and I, along with Bob and his business partner, threw ourselves into the project. The aft hatch was sealed, teak toe rails were removed, and the bottom was sanded till smooth as a baby's bottom. When the boat was ready to be sailed, we raced the boat we named *Vanishing Girl* successfully, leaving most of our competition in the dust.

In a race held off the Ventura coastline, I fell overboard. It was a windy day with a lot of wave action. Our boat had just rounded the leeward mark, and I was late pulling down the spinnaker. Bob was putting the boat into a hard tack to go back to weather. While scrambling to get the spinnaker put away, I got wrapped around the large fluffy sail—lines and all. I slid off the deck and was thrown into the water, a submerged sausage, unable to move my arms and legs. A crew member shouted off the stern of our boat, "Man overboard!" to the two boats that were right on our tail. If I had not been tangled into a web of lines that were attached to the boat, I could have been run over by hard-charging race boats that were just feet away. Walt and Bob were able to lean over the side of the boat and grab me and the spinnaker. They threw the whole wad—me and the sail—into the cockpit. I was waterlogged but okay, except for my damaged ego. After a lot of scrambling to undo the mess I had made, we were on our way to the windward mark, with big smiles on our faces. Bob told me, "We have to finish the race with the same number of people we started with, so stay on the boat, Mom." (My son calls me Sal, except when the subject is serious).

A few months later, we discussed the potential of *Vanishing Girl* and contemplated redesigning the boat to be lighter and faster. After debating the effort it was another go! Walt and I funded the project; Bob directed it. He chose Carl Schumacher, a naval architect, to draw up sail and boat plans that would balance the keel and rig's center of gravity from specifications he and Walt laid out. Dennis Choate, a naval architect and boatbuilder, was chosen to build our elliptical rudder. Ballenger and Omahundra, both component designers and builders, would build us a carbon-fiber boom and mast.

When our plans took shape, we met Bob at the farmhouse in Oxnard where he had taken *Vanishing Girl* for the redesign. The farm had acres of land, including a large shed and a big cement side yard. The property was owned by the family of one of Bob's surfing buddies.

Bob had completely dismantled the boat, down to the bare hull, and was sawing off the keel as we pulled up in our car. At this

|Vanishing Girl prior to rebuild|

stage, it was necessary to brace the sides of the boat with a two-by-four to keep the hull from collapsing in on itself.

|Boat-building project begins|

The three of us designed, built, and installed new lightweight foam ring frames. We fiberglassed them into place, then sanded the ring frames to smoothly conform into the hull.

|*Sanding new ring frames*|

Bob cut away the old boat deck with a Sawzall and threw it in the trash.

A cockpit mold was built out of door skins. This pattern would radically change the cockpit design, taking away the seating area. We should have bought stock in the fiberglass, sandpaper, and resin industries. Our monthly bill from Port Supply, a discount marine store, was astronomical!

|*New cockpit design*|

Next we vacuum-bagged the new cockpit. Bob had never vacuum-bagged, and Walt and I had never heard of the process. This is a delicate undertaking. Fiberglass and foam were laid over the curving sixteen-by-eight-foot door skin cockpit mold. Resin was slathered over the fiberglass and covered with plastic sheeting. The tricky part was getting a perfect seal around the perimeter, before the resin "started to cook." Walt and Bob devised a pump to suck out the air between the plastic sheeting and the fiberglass and resin. After a lot of sweat and labor, the sealing procedure worked. We gave each other a high five and had a cold one.

We carefully pulled the new cockpit away from the mold, then gingerly brought it over to the boat. It was a fit. Prolific sanding was an understatement. I had to tape my fingers so that sanding did not make them bleed.

Walt and I met Bob at the boat on Tuesday and Thursday evenings after work and Saturday mornings. Bob brought a list of projects to complete that day. I brought the sandwiches. Walt was the project's mathematician. Every work session brought new challenges. This routine lasted three and a half years.

Delays and screwups during construction were common. However, we pulled together and got through it, actually enjoying the work, and looked forward to going over to the farmhouse to work on the "girl."

Using ropes and pulleys that were attached to an overhead boatyard hoist, we raised the boat high enough to accommodate a 180-degree roll and turned her over. This process was repeated five times, at different intervals, to sand and work on the keel stub and boat bottom. For a bunch of amateurs, we were doing a fantastic job, thanks to our bank account, Bob's expertise, and our team's dedication and hard work to accomplish our goal.

|Rolling the boat over to work on the bottom|

The Schumacher-designed bulb keel was delivered to the farmyard. We ordered it from a Northern California keel company. After delivery, we started sanding and shaping her. Bob was concerned that the J-hooks, which went deep into the keel, were not placed correctly. It turned out that two of the J-hooks would have entered the ring frame, instead of the boat bottom. (The top of the j-hooks were threaded, ready to be bolted through the boat bottom.)

The "Aqua-net 22" metal in the J-hooks has the specialized ability to retain memory, which enabled the keel to move slightly when the boat was under harsh sailing conditions, then move back to its original form.

We contacted the keel manufacturer. The owner of the company was off snow skiing but called us back. He was upset the error had occurred and had a flatbed truck sent to our little boatyard to pick up the screwed-up keel.

Our lead keel was melted down in the ultrasecret keel factory (lead is an environmental nightmare in California) and the J-hooks were properly placed. When the keel was redelivered to us, we started sanding it again.

It was time to attach the keel to the boat bottom. Bob and Walt pulled the chain hoist to the top of the rig so that the boat was far enough off the ground to clear the area where the five-foot-deep keel had to be attached. Penciled-out holes in the boat bottom's stub showed where to place the drill bit. While Bob drilled and drilled, I pushed his arms up higher and higher, as he painstakingly pushed the three-foot-long drill up through the

|*Long-boarding the keel*|

fiberglass hull. Walt held a plumb bob at the bow to guide us. That job finished, we wheeled the keel stand, holding our bright and shiny keel, under the holes. All six J-hooks seamlessly slid into place. Heavy-duty nuts secured the keel to the boat. It was time to stand back and revel in our success.

As the boat began to take shape, sailing friends stopped by to ooh and ah over the state-of-the-art racing machine being built.

The new elliptical rudder was installed without a hitch. It was now time to trailer the boat from the farmhouse to a commercial boatyard to get our pride and joy spray-painted.

|*It's a perfect fit*|

We pulled *Vanishing Girl* to Stanton's Boat Yard in the Ventura Marina.

The deck was painted brilliant white, and the sides "Stars and Stripes" blue. *Wow!* We stared in amazement at her beauty.

The next phase was to take the boat to her new home, the Ventura Yacht Club, to install the eye candy (rigging).

Getting the new carbon-fiber mast proved to be a challenge. One spar company, Omahundra, made carbon-fiber masts, and we were last in line, because the bigger seventy- to one-hundred-footers took priority over our little thirty-four-foot spar. This was the year (1994) that the America's Cup was being sailed off the San Diego coastline. Every boat in the race wanted one of the newly designed lightweight masts.

Our new spar was finally delivered on a rainy February afternoon. Walt and Bob set it up on sawhorses so we could start pulling the halyards through the innards of the mast.

It became evident that the "tangs" at the top of the mast were ill-placed. Not wanting to drill into carbon fiber, we thought it prudent to have a factory guy come out and redo the holes where the halyards feed into the masthead. Progress was stopped. We impatiently stomped around our work site. The factory rep turned out to be a good guy and very helpful. He fixed our problem.

Now we could proceed with the fun stuff. Every block, winch, lifeline, turnbuckle, pulley, and halyard we installed on the boat

|*Installing carbon-fiber mast*|

made it look snazzier. Our friend and crew member, Gy, built an awesome black anodized aluminum mast step in his machine shop (Gy's company designs and builds high-tech specialty parts). He engraved *Vanishing Girl* into the base of the step. The guys installed this work of art below deck. It held our mast in place. All our sailing buddies watched our progress, climbing the stepladder up to the cockpit to give their two cents' worth of advice while we worked away.

Just sitting on the trailer in the yacht club parking lot, *Vanishing Girl* looked like a fast boat.

The big day was here; it was time to launch the girl! Bob pulled the trailer over to the hoist and gingerly connected the lifting-eye down through the cabin opening to the keel bolts.

Walt had a line off the bow; I had a line off the stern, and Bob was controlling the hoist to get the boat over the water and to slowly lower it.

Walt was so intent on watching the bow come around that he stepped off the end of the dock and fell into the water. We laughed. Our built-up tensions dissipated.

After three and a half years of redesign, our boat was finally in the water, and, boy, did she ever look pretty! We hoisted *Vanishing Girl*'s brand-new sails and took off down Ventura Harbor and out into the ocean.

The wind was about five knots, but the boat pulled forward as if it had wings. We had taken one thousand pounds of weight out of her, went up four and a half feet on the mast, increased the sail area by 40 percent, and the elliptical rudder was a foot deeper. The original fat, stubby keel was now a long, thin, deeper keel with a bulb on the bottom. The cockpit was a sixteen-foot "working" cockpit, so the crew could move from side to side with ease. We had a full-roach main with running backstays (no supporting cable attached to the top of the mast). The mainsail was huge!

|*Vanishing Girl's first sail after rebuild*|

We took turns at the helm as Bob made adjustments to the sails and tried out all the "go-fast" rigging apparatus. A six-pack of beer was passed around, and you could not wipe the big smiles off our faces!

Our team entered regattas and other local races, winning most because of Bob's sailing ability and "light is right" "go-fast" philosophy. He does not have crew that can't perform. Walt and I worked hard on the boat, crewing on most of the races. In light-air races we screamed—heavy-air races were wet and wild.

|*Bob driving Vanishing Girl on a beat to weather. The crew is rail-meat in between tacks. Credit for photograph is given to gericonser@earthlink.net.*|

Every year Santa Barbara Yacht Club and the King-Harbor Yacht Club sponsor a race down the coast from Santa Barbara, taking Anacapa Island to port, and finishing in King Harbor. This was a favorite race and one in which we always did well. Geri Conser's aerial photography company took some impressive photos of our boat during this race.

|*Racing down the California coastline. Credit for photograph given to gericonser@earthlink.net.*|

After a couple of years racing *Vanishing Girl*, Walt's work, our hectic schedule, and Bob sailing in the big-boat racing circuit, determined our decision to put our pride and joy on the market.

|*Surfing the waves. Credit for photograph is given to gericonser@earthlink.net.*|

We sold the boat to a guy who lived in Santa Cruz, California. He had a difficult time racing the boat. Winds are much stronger up north than they are in Southern California. The girl was too much for him. The boat was grounded in a race when his sailing crew could not stop *Vanishing Girl* from sailing wildly straight into the beach.

Bob's most recent races were aboard a well-known seventy-two-foot carbon-fiber racing machine called *Peligrosso*. The boat entered long-distance races to Mexico and Hawaii. A few years ago, he sailed his twenty-first Trans-Pac Race. In the middle of that race, he witnessed a catamaran horizon their monohull. Bob became a multihull convert, proclaiming, "There are dogs, and there are cats."

Catamarans are much faster than monohulls because of their lightness, and their narrow and shallow hulls that skim the water, producing less drag than a monohull. Bob and his friend Hank bought a thirty-six-foot cat that had been setting in a boatyard for a long time. It was mouldy and rusty. They refurbished the cat they named *Two of Ten*, bringing her up to race-ready standards. After a year and a half of hard work, the boat was ready. Bob and Hank threw a party at their shop in Ventura. Beer, food, and a band to dance the night away made this celebratory event a blast. Their boat sat on a trailer in the middle of the parking lot party.

Next step, trailer the boat down to Channel Islands Harbor, lash the mesh decking between the hulls, launch her, and then step the mast. Bob, Hank, and Walt made sure all the catamaran parts fit into place and were securely fastened. I, again, was the gofer.

Walt and I got to sail on *Two Of Ten* several times. It quickly picks up velocity, surfs over waves, and can sustain speeds of thirty-five knots for as long as the crew can hang on. Blasting downwind has the effect of a firehose shooting cold saltwater in your face. Sailing on the cat was an experience for which all the "hot" sailors stood in line.

The two guys had a superb time racing her, learning new ways to set records down the coast and around the race course.

Ocean Kayaking

Anacapa Island is thirteen miles off the coast of Channel Islands Harbor. Walt and I set out with a group of kayakers to paddle across the open ocean to this national park. We were far from expert kayakers. The sun shone brightly—there was just a whiff of wind. We had food and camping gear packed in our waterproof hatches. During the crossing, our hands became numb from clinching our paddles too hard. The five-hour crossing was a long time to sit in a kayak seat. We cautiously crossed the shipping lane and windy lane, both on our pathway to the island. The rocky shoreline of the island finally came into view. Once we tucked our kayaks into the cove by the Anacapa Lighthouse, we were able to grab the railing of the seventy-four steps that lead to the top of the island. Our kayaks were stored on a ramp, and we took our sleeping bags and sandwiches up to a little campground that was in the middle of a bird rookery. The view was stupendious.

From our lofty perch, we watched the sun set on the backside of Santa Cruz Island. The next morning we watched the sun rise over the Santa Monica Mountains. Our sore hands had to get us back to the mainland the next day. By the time we paddled back to Channel Islands Harbor, we had figured out the correct way of paddling, putting our full upper bodies into the effort of each stroke of the kayak paddle. We had managed to not tip our kayaks over and handled the rolling ocean waves. Our kayaks were not very seaworthy, and we lucked out that pleasant weather stayed with us all weekend. This was an extremely fun-filled adventure.

Evening and weekend paddles in the waters off the coast of Channel Islands was making us become accomplished kayakers. Walt and I rented a sailboat to take out to Santa Cruz Island for the weekend. We tied our kayaks on deck and took off for the backside of the island, to Albert's Cove. The weather was sunny and warm. Six hours later we anchored our boat in the cove and paddled our kayaks through the waves to shore—we ate, drank, kayaked, hiked hills overlooking the ocean horizon, and watched the sun set over the island while anchored in our little paradise. Outdoor fun is everything it's cracked up to be!

|*Santa Cruz Island kayak landing*|

A group of kayaking buddies joined Walt and me for another weekend getaway. We camped near San Simeon Castle, north of Morro Bay, and launched our kayaks next to the pier. The day was warm, bright, and sunny—unusual for this fog-prone coastline, where the wind whips the sea into frothy foam. We paddled about three miles out to sea, and then headed north toward the Point Piedras Blancas Lighthouse. The ocean view of the San Simeon Castle kept me mesmorized. I didn't see the giant rock protrusion ahead of us until there was a lot of splashing around the kayaks. Seals were using the rock to slide into the water, do flips, and wattle around on. It was a hilarious scene. We were still a few miles south of our goal, so put full effort into paddling fast. Approaching the lighthouse, we spied elephant seals on the beach. I was intrigued and paddled closer to shore. Walt was yelling for me to turn back.

I kept easing my way into shore. The seals were flipping sand over their bodies with one of their flippers to cool themselves. They were in a resting position and didn't look threatening. I beached my kayak, got out, and walked among the giant beasts, looking at them eye to eye. Turning my back on them seemed risky, so I slowly walked backward to my kayak, got in, and paddled out to sea. No one in our group thought this was a smart action on my part, but I was glowing inside.

Shuttle Launch

Walt had scheduled business trips to Cape Canaveral to work with the air force space programs quite often. I traveled with him on some of these trips and really lucked out when there was a shuttle launch while we were holed up in Coco Beach. Walt had a meeting, but some of his workmates took me out to the area where the launch takes place. At T-minus ten the whole site started to rock and roll. Great billows of smoke came out of the rocket platform as the coundown continued over a loudspeaker. At T-minus one, fire came out of the rocket tail. The space capsule blasted off with a mighty roar. A crackling could be heard as the rocket soared for the heavens. The impressive hunk of metal did a 180-degree roll and quickly rose out of sight. *Wow!* What a phenomenal experience to witness the power of a space launch.

We were still in Coco Beach seven days later. I stood on a picnic table at our hotel and was able to see the shuttle come back to earth and land. This was a eureka moment.

Annapolis, Maryland

Walt's employer, the Aerospace Corporation, is a think tank for space-related projects. Its main customer is the United States Air Force. The company is based in El Segundo, California, on the Los

Angeles Air Force Base. Its ratio of people with advanced degrees is high.

The non-DOD (Department of Defense) business office is located in Washington, DC. Walt had an opportunity to transfer back to the East Coast office in 1995. We thought it might be fun to live back east for a few years and experience the culture and history of the area, so we sold our condo in Channel Islands Harbor, packed up, and moved east. We had a hiatus from sailing.

The winter of 1995-96 was one of the worst on record. We arrived in Annapolis, Maryland, in November to look for a house, our worldly goods in storage. It was cold and snowing.

We found a beautiful home in Riva, Maryland, southwest of Annapolis, on the South River. The upstairs master suite had a step-up Jacuzzi with skylights and a beautiful mahogany arch-framed window over the tub. We loved to sit in the hot bubbles under candlelight while storms raged outside, watching tops of our one-hundred-foot trees bow in the wind. The house was huge--library, living room, formal dining room, large kitchen with a family room and fireplace, three staircases, and a full basement. Walt and I spent an inordinate amount of time trying to find each other.

East Coast houses are roomy because they are a refuge in the winter from nasty weather. The house was situated on an acre, with scores of trees and a giant lawn area.

We were used to living in a little condominium on the beach, with no yard. The local furniture store in Annapolis helped fill the rooms. We built a garden shed to put our new John Deere lawn mower in, along with other tools necessary to maintain the place—most of which we were unfamiliar with.

The backyard reminded us of campgrounds we had stayed in, so we thought it a good idea to build a fire pit in the middle of our little forest. It turned out to be a great place to meet the neighbors, who smelled the fire and brought a bottle of wine over and asked to join us.

Heart Surgery

Our bliss lasted until February of 1996, when Walt was shoveling snow out in the driveway. He came into the house, sat down in a chair, and announced his chest hurt. We made an appointment with a cardiologist, who sat up a stress treadmill test.

The results showed there was a heart blockage, so an angiogram was scheduled. The doctor said Walt had an occlusion in a main artery. An angioplasty was necessary. The blockage was pulled out through his veins. It looked like a small piece of pasta. The next day he was fine and was released from the hospital.

Now that Walt was all fixed up, I was again having angina. After tests, the cardiologist said I had a "global" problem where the majority of my arteries were clogged. I was scheduled for open-heart surgery.

Heart bypass surgery is extremely invasive and can cause a multitude of serious complications, systemic in nature. Fortunately, most people go through this operation with no side effects. However, a few of us aren't so lucky.

At sixty-three, I continued to be small in stature. My cholesterol was low, with a one to one ratio of HDL/LDL. However, an elevated Lipoprotein(a) caused my arterial disorder. This is a particularly pernicious artery-clogging cholesterol. A healthy diet and exercise does not stop its progress. Doctors told us the disease is inherited. I had not heard of anyone in my family with heart problems, except for my dad's brother. Niacin is the only heart medication that helps lower LP(a).

During this surgery, doctors sawed my chest open and put me on a heart machine so they can disconnect my heart from the diseased arteries that needed to be removed. Veins were taken from my right leg along with mammary glands from my chest. Four clogged arteries were removed from my heart.

The surgeon was a big guy, over six feet tall. His large hands must have had a difficult time working inside of my small chest cavity. He accidentally clipped the nerve going to my diaphragm. This caused my system to lose its ability to maintain aerobic capacity when I exercise. I immediately go anaerobic—I can only swim one length of the pool before resting, where I could swim two and a half miles without stopping before the bypass.

After surgery, I arrived in the recovery area in critical condition. The next morning, which was on a Saturday, I was told by the nursing staff in recovery that they did not work on weekends. I was holding up their exit. There was no way to speak because of the breathing tube. Lying in a prone position, not able to move, I tried writing "sick" on a tablet. The codeine going into my veins was causing me to be nauseated.

Saturday afternoon, over twenty-four hours after surgery, my lungs were not yet reoxygenated. The breathing tube inserted down my throat couldn't be removed. It was evening when a nurse said I could now safely have the tube pulled out. The whole experience was horrible.

After a week in the hospital, all the tubes were gone, and recovery started. It was later discovered I had suffered a stroke during surgery.

A few days after I returned home pericarditis (an inflammation of the heart sac) developed and took me down like a sledgehammer. Doctors assured me that it lasted only a few days, or two weeks at max. This incapacitating condition lasted six months.

I was placed on the steroid Prednisone. If I tried to walk, I went into atrial fibrillation. Emergency care and hospitalization were frequently required.

My wonderful, loving husband carried me, pushed me in the wheelchair, and took care of my gazillion needs, all while driving to Washington, DC, to go to work.

The Prednisone drove me nuts! Not being able to be physical, my mind was in overdrive. I read articles on countries in *National Geographic* magazines, and read history, science, philosophy, and political works, and wrote my interpretations down for Walt to read, not that he had the time. He said my reports didn't make any sense. I erroneously thought they were intellectually wonderful.

My battered health was taking its toll on our lives. Living in a part of the country that was foreign to us, where we had no family or close friends, caused us to be terribly homesick.

We missed California. I felt that if I could see Bob and our friends around Channel Islands Harbor and the Colorado River it could soothe my soul and make my body whole again.

We flew from Baltimore to LAX. The flight was difficult. I was weak and oxygen starved and not smart enough to ask for oxygen on the airplane.

We stayed with friends who lived near the airport that night and drove to the Colorado River the next day. I was exhausted. We stayed with our friends Jack and Linda. Jack gave me a lawn chair to relax my weary bones in while I soaked up the warm sun and watched the river flow by. Suddenly, I went into "a fib" big time. Walt frantically drove me to the hospital. Doctors and nurses hovered over me and pulled me through. They kept me overnight. I thought I was okay when I was released from the hospital, so the next day we headed west toward Channel Islands Harbor.

Our friend John had a welcoming party for us and invited our sailing friends. In the middle of the party, I again went into "a fib." Off to the hospital for another session of gut-wrenching hysteria, as another medical team worked on me.

My cardiologist in Annapolis gave us strict orders to get on the next plane back to Maryland. Walt and I never got to spend any quality time with Bob. The flight back was easier because I sucked on an oxygen bottle the whole way.

A year and a half later, after experiencing East Coast history, culture, and being ill, we decided to move back to Channel Islands Harbor. Walt's employer was obliging and transferred him back to its El Segundo location.

We flew to Los Angeles to go house hunting. While driving north along the sun-drenched beach scenery on Highway 1 in Santa Monica, we stopped for a red light. A bikini-clad young woman was roller-skating across the highway in front of us. A guy in a pickup truck was turning left. The woman was in his way. He called out, "Bitch, move it!" She gave him the finger! Walt and I gave each other a high five and knew we had returned home to kooky, wonderful, warm Southern California.

The flight back to Annapolis to finalize the sale of our home was the end of our East Coast stint. Our heads were spinning, just thinking about living next to the Pacific Ocean again.

On the day escrow closed, our possessions were put in a moving van, and we headed west in our motor home, visiting the last of the fifty states I had not yet seen.

Traveling across the Flatlands was monotonous. The beauty of the Rockies woke us up. Just south of Arches National Park in eastern Utah is Moab, a town known for extreme mountain biking and river-raft trips. We didn't have to look far to find a raft trip down the Green River, through the confluence of the Green and Colorado Rivers, ending up at the head of Lake Powell. Our small group of river rafters crashed through twenty-five sets of rapids during the next four days. The river guides were young action-packed studs. They cooked scrumptious meals on sandy beaches and took us on hikes every evening into caves and up escarpments that overlooked the beautiful canyons through which we were rafting. At night we slept in our sleeping bags under the stars. However, when we woke up in the morning, no one was ever within range of Walt's loud snoring. The group of people we were with complained mightily that it was impossible to get any sleep if they were unlucky enough to plop a sleeping bag anywhere close to ours. (Walt's snoring didn't bother me.) Big rapids required wet suits and double life jackets. We bounced through them and wanted more. By the time we reached our take-out point, everyone in our group was bosom buddies with each other and our guides. Gargantuan caves and rock formations at the head of Lake Powell look like a paintbrush sculpted the vibrant colors. We hiked through red, orange, and brown molded caverns in awe of the smooth weather-worn-curved surface. A small plane took us back to Moab, twisting and turning over the river and canyons we had just traversed.

Return to the Beach from Maryland

Entering eastern California, Walt and I stopped off at our favorite spot on the Colorado River, a small development where you tie up a kayak or ski boat on your own beach, and have off-road access to the desert mountains and washes. One of the undeveloped lots at the north end of the community had a for-sale sign planted in the dirt. A waterfront lot was more than we had contemplated, but we thought it worth the price, so we purchased a sublease. The property is on Indian land.

I had been going to the river to water ski long before I met Walt. This is in a remote area right in the middle of the low desert, where it gets blazin' hot in the summer and pleasantly beautiful during the rest of the year.

Escrow was opened. To celebrate that evening we drove a friend's dunebuggy down a desert wash and gathered a bunch of dead branches from mesquite and palo verde trees, piled them on top of the buggy, took them back to our newly purchased lot, and built a huge fire.

It was New Year's Eve, the end of 1997. The beer flowed, and we danced around the fire. A light was on in the neighbor to the south's home, so I went over and banged on his door. A young man opened the door, with a big smile on his face. I told him we had just purchased the lot next to him, and we were celebrating. Would he care to join us? His answer, "Hell yes!" It was the beginning of an ongoing close friendship with Matt. He lives in

Orange County and owns his own business. His river house is his getaway weekend pad.

Walt and I left the river, continuing to drive west, back to our old stomping grounds and new home in Channel Islands Harbor. The townhome we bought is on a narrow peninsula between the small boat harbor and the ocean. Our new home came with a forty-foot dock that was more than ample to store our fourteen-foot kayaks. Our neighbors had oceangoing power or sail boats tied up in front of their houses. The back channel, where our house was located, was just off the main harbor channel. Anacapa Island and Santa Cruz Island were in line with the sun, as it set off our coastline.

It sure felt good to be in familiar beach territory. Our new home needed revitalization. We gutted the interior and brought the house into top condition. The only downside was living sixty miles north of Walt's work. He spent a lot of time driving up and down the Coast Highway (we had been here before).

A scan of my brain during a check-up at a cardiologist's office in Ventura showed why my system had not recovered from the bypass surgery. I had suffered a stroke during that surgery, which caused the pituitary gland to malfunction.

This is the master endocrine gland, affecting all hormonal functions of the body. Blood tests showed that my cholesterol was, as the doctor said, lower than that of a dying cancer patient. My whole system was out of whack. A simple once a day thyroid pill was needed to bring me back to health. The medication immediately altered my physical health in a positive way. I felt strong and raring to go—back to normal!

Whistler Ski Trip

A group of friends asked us to join them on a snow skiing trip to Whistler Mountain Ski Resort, north of Vancouver, Canada. We packed our ski clothes and headed for the airport.

In order to avoid another calamity like he had in Park City, Walt took ski lessons. This worked out fine. He was doing great, and I was having a wonderful time gliding down the mountain on the new parabolic skis. However, on the third day out, it snowed heavily, and we decided to go snowmobiling with our friends.

Walt and I rode on the same snowmobile—not a good decision—and we took turns driving. The heavily laden snowy forests and meadows made for a delightful afternoon of going lickety-split over a soft terrain. I drove over a little woop-dee-do, and Walt fell off the back. The snowmobile fell over and landed on his ankle, breaking the same leg he had broken six years earlier. Walt was again put in a basket and taken to the nearest emergency facility by the ski patrol. Another leg surgery was needed, with pins and plates installed into the ankle, but it could wait until we got back to California, so we gave away our lift tickets to our skiing buddies and drove to the airport, and Walt had another uncomfortable airplane ride home with another broken leg.

River Abode

Good old disability insurance! After surgery, Walt was on crutches for a couple of months, which meant we were able to spend a lot of time overseeing our new place in the desert. Water, sewer, propane, and electric lines were buried underground on our lot site.

The day the big event occurred (arrival of new house), Walt sat on our neighbor's porch with his foot up in the air. I kept an eye peeled for any action on the entrance road to our lot. The weather was warm and beautiful. Ron landed his boat on our beach and asked if I wanted to go waterskiing. You bet! He pulled me upriver a few miles, then turned around and brought me back. I did a double take when we got close to our lot. Two roofs were moving down the road. I knew it was our new mobile home! Walt was waving his crutches at me. I let go of the ski rope, skied onto the beach, and ran up the grass barefoot to be with Walt so we could coordinate where the two trucks should plant our home. Walt and I watched as the work crew joined the two sections of the nifty, brand-new sixty-six-by-twenty-eight-foot mobile home together.

|*Waterskiing on the Colorado River—pure ecstasy*|:

After three days of pushing and shoving, our mobile became one big unit. Supports were put under the mobile, and the wheels were removed. We were then allowed to go inside to inspect our new home away from home. Mountains can be seen out our bedroom and bathroom windows, and the Colorado River flows by our kitchen windows and the two french doors in our living room. Desert is all around us. Mountain ranges are visible in every direction.

We had a garage built, which is offset to retain the mountain view out our windows. Contractors poured a cement driveway and patio. Landscaping came later.

We drove from Channel Islands to the river for our first weekend stay at our river digs, with great expectations of a glorious experience. The utilities were connected. A quick stop to get groceries and a new barbecue was the last chore.

The weather was gorgeous. Walt sat up a couple of beach chairs on the patio and poured us a glass of wine, while we waited for the barbecue to heat up so we could cook dinner. One glass of wine turned into two, but the fire would not start. We didn't mind; the river was flowing by, and we were in paradise. When the stars came out, hunger pangs took over, and we brought the meat inside and cooked it on the stove.

The next morning the cement guys came to finish up our sidewalk project. We heard them outside in a knee-slappin' howl. They were holding up the bag of "ceramic charcoal" we had purchased to cook dinner. They thought the story about our misadventure the night before was hilarious. We laughed pretty hard too!

We now owned a home next to the ocean, where we sailed, mountain biked, ran on the beach, and kayaked, and a place on the river, where we ran, kayaked, water-skied, and played in the desert.

Desert exploration is limited to the wintertime—it's too frickin' hot to climb hills and negotiate washes when the sun is scorching and unmercifully burning through you. Walt and I tried this sport during our Christmas/New Year's vacation break. Ron loaned us one of his dunebuggies. It was in questionable shape. Some of the wheel lug bolts were missing, and one of the big back tires was on the front, with the little tire on the back, because the lug bolts didn't match where the tires belonged. A run through the desert landscape of palo verde and mesquite trees, creosote bushes, thorny cactus plants, rocky plateaus, and sandy washes took us to an old western bar (that has since burned down). After shooting pool and drinking a beer, we were ready to head back home. Our tires were low, and we had lost a couple more lug bolts. All the guys in our group told Walt to hit the gas and not let the buggy sink into the sand. He hit a corner too fast about halfway home; the buggy spun out and turned over. We came to a stop upside down, dangling from our four-point harnesses. Another buggy came by—the guys on board released us from our predicament. My leg had a gash in it, but otherwise we were in one piece. We were kidded a lot about being novices in the desert.

British Virgin Islands

Opportunities to do bareboat charters in the Caribbean were not passed up. Our first trip was flying to the British Virgins and renting three Morgan forty-one-foot sailboats. Two couples were on each boat. A fun group of friends that we sailed with in the Ventura area joined us. Our scuba diving friend Josh and his girlfriend Lillian were our shipmates. Trouble was brewing while we were putting provisions aboard our boat. Lillian was upset that another girlfriend of Josh's was joining him the second week of the trip. Lillian was staying the first week. She had found out about this arrangement at a ski club social event the week before. I asked her why she came when she knew about the plan. She mumbled something unintelligible, and then went into a tirade about how Josh was treating her. I told her she had two choices: leave the boat and fly home or stop griping and enjoy the adventure. No one on our boat or the other two boats wanted her complaining about how her perceived boyfriend was treating her.

Lillian decided to stay. During the next week she tried every trick imaginable to get Josh to fall in love with her (Josh was in love with Lisa—the second week's pick). Lillian lit candles in the evening and rubbed Josh down with perfumed massage oil and waited on him hand and foot. Josh was being rebellious and didn't shave the whole week.

The British Virgin Islands are close together and only take a couple of hours of sailing to island hop. The first night out we anchored in front of "Sydney's Peace & Love Restaurant." It had an open bar with a coffee can to put money in for the drinks we poured. We sat at picnic tables and ordered lobster. Lively music played in the background. We danced, jumped in the water to try standing up on our windsurfer, and ate lobster. None of us were getting the hang of windsurfing, but, luckily, the wind was light, and we didn't crash into other boats.

Virgin Gorda is a great skin diving stopover. The water is blue-green, with deep clarity. This is a lovely spot to see multitudes of colorful fish and horse around under the water.

Tortola has a large anchorage. We anchored our boats offshore and swam ashore to partake in cocktails called "Sun-downers" at a beach bar. A steel drum band played while we danced on the beach to the beat.

St. John's and St. Thomas were a blur. We found a rum distillery that manufactured rotgut rum and sold it to unsuspecting patrons (us). Fishing was productive. We ate lots of different fish that were cleaned and cooked in our galley. A woman on a nearby anchored boat rowed her dinghy over to our three anchored boats to see if any of the women in our group wanted to buy little sun outfits from her. I bought three. She then proceeded to tell us that some of the local fish were poisonous. We had prepared various kinds of fish for dinner. Since we didn't know what kind they were, we threw them overboard and cooked spaghetti.

Josh took Lillian to the airport. She carried several bottles of rotgut rum back home for Josh. He shaved. Lisa came off the plane that Lillian boarded. There was a lot of snickering between us and our sailing friends about Josh's shenanigans.

By the time our trip was over, we were all planning our next Caribbean bareboat charter.

President's Escapade

Walt and I hardly had time to watch the news. However, the political scene was starting to get interesting. President Clinton had been elected to a second term, aided by a booming economy. However, his office became mired in "character" issues—the Whitewater land deal and sexual misconduct.

In January 1998, Bill Clinton denied, under oath, that he had a sexual affair with White House intern Monica Lewinsky and had tried to cover it up. Lewinsky's dress proved to be Clinton's downfall. It had his semen on it.

In August, Clinton made history by becoming the first US president to testify in front of a grand jury in an investigation of his own possibly criminal conduct.

In an address to the nation, he admitted to having had an inappropriate relationship with Lewinsky, who publicized the intimate details of the affair.

After an exhaustive investigation, the White House independent counsel, Kenneth Starr, delivered his report on the Clinton investigation to the House of Representatives. It outlined eleven different grounds for impeachment. The main focus was Clinton's moral conduct, graphically detailing his corrupt behavior.

On December 19, 1998, Clinton became the second American president to be impeached. After a Senate trial in early 1999, Clinton was acquitted, because he had a Democratic majority in Congress.

President Clinton left office with a budget surplus.

His sexual misconduct ruined his reputation for the foreseeable future. He had dishonored the presidency.

Windward Islands

It was time to sail away again, this time to the Windward Islands, north of Granada. Four couples joined us to sail a fifty-foot French-built Benito sailing sloop from island to island. The trip started off rough. While sitting aboard a plane waiting to take off from our layover stop in Dallas, the flight attendant came down the aisle and asked Walt to deplane with her. We both jumped out of our seats to find out what the ruckus was. A phone call from Walt's secretary to the airline said Walt's mom had passed away. He called his sister and explained that we were en route to St. Lucia in the Carribean. Six other people on the plane were dependent upon us for the trip because I was the captain of the boat we were sailing.

No one else had the bona fides to qualify for sailing the fifty-foot vessel. His sister was incensed and has never forgiven us for not attending his mom's funeral. Walt was not close to his mom. He had been through enormous pain associated with her past depraved behavior. We got back on the plane, and off we flew.

Our boat sailed away from St. Lucia, heading south. Islands in this vicinity are far apart. I was looking for wind to get a rail under and spray coming over the deck. This boat could haul in a breeze. Unfortunately, we had light wind. Another unfortunate circumstance was that each island was a different country, which meant that we had to enter and exit customs often. Walt and I stood in line at various custom offices while the rest of the party hit the local bars.

Mistique, the isle of the rich and famous (the queen of England has a residence here), has exclusive hotels and restaurants. We hitched a ride with a local tour guide that took us into a few of the islands sumptious dwellings. He also sold live lobsters. Walt gave the guy the shirt he was wearing, plus money. He and Jack competed to see who could buy the most bugs. That evening, while sitting at anchor, the lobsters were cleaned and boiled. The stern of the boat was filled with black lobster juice--upcoming menues included a wide variety of lobster dishes.

As the evening grew more riotious, Walt decided to hold a wake for his mom. We joined in with abandon, singing salty sea songs and howling at the moon. The next day was less stressful for Walt. He felt he had justly dealt with his grief.

Freshwater supplies aboard our boat seemed low. A couple of us had filled gallon jugs with tap water and placed them in the bilge for an emergency supply. Some of the women were taking long showers and letting the faucet on the galley sink run endlessly.

Palm Island is a picture-perfect paradise—swaying palm trees, white sandy beaches, and an endless breaking surf along the shoreline—music to our ears. The sea was rolling, however, we were securely anchored offshore. I wanted to stay here all night but was voted down by those that thought we should pull anchor and head for St. Vincent Island (a trash heap poverty-ridden piece of dirt a few miles to the west) to get more water. Upon entering St. Vincent's boat harbor a Pongo row boat came close to us. He accused us of sinking his boat. We didn't give him the money he was demanding. He and his dilapidated boat were fine. We backed our boat into a spot where we could reach a freshwater hose and let her rip.

Early the next morning we turned the boat north to sail back to St. Lucia. When we docked, the boat rental guys wanted to know why all the jugs of water were in the bilge.

CHAPTER 8

Getting Back Up after Bike Accident; 9/11 Attack; Colorado

My health had been exceptional during the last six months. I was able to go on some gnarly mountain bike rides; running on the beach was fun; water-skiing at the river was awesome, and we sailed out to Santa Cruz Island often, our kayaks in tow.

Outdoor fun was about to end. On an early summer morning in August of 1999, I went mountain biking with our friend Scott in Sycamore Canyon. This mountainous area is on the southern edge of Ventura County, and it butts up to the coast. It is California State Park land, chock-full of steep bike climbs and fast downhills over rocks, narrow dirt trails, and water crossings. Wildflowers cover the ground, interspersed with gigantic oak trees.

Scott and I were riding through some muddy trails. I biked down a hill into a water crossing, hit a rock with my front wheel, and flipped over the handlebars of my bike headfirst, hitting a rock.

I lay in the dirt. When I became aware that I could not move, I asked Scott if my legs were still in the air. That's where they were when I heard my neck crack on the rock I was propelled into. He said my legs were on the ground. I couldn't feel or move my body, and I thought, *Life is over, as I know it.* I was paralyzed.

Neither of us had cell phones with us, so Scott biked off to find a forest ranger to send in help. Mountain lions roam the surrounding hills. I was easy prey. It was Monday. No other bikers or hikers came by. Scott led a medical team back up the trail. It took them about forty minutes to reach me, and when they did they could detect very faint vital signs.

A rescue helicopter arrived on the scene and flew me to St. John's Hospital in Oxnard. I was in a semiconscious state during the flight but remember screaming because my body was in a violent spasm.

Scott called Walt at work, who was at an off-site meeting. Walt's secretary reached him by telephone to tell him I had been in a traffic accident, and my legs were crushed. How stories get confused! Walt frantically drove to the hospital from Los Angeles.

There was a terrific summer storm that night, with lightning and thunder. I was unconscious and in the MRI machine. Every time the technicians got me inside the machine, electric power quit. They knew I had bruised my spinal column at the C-3 and C-4 level. It took all night to complete the scan.

Sensation returned to my limbs the next day. However, my right arm and leg didn't work. I was put into the nonambulatory rehab floor of St. John's Hospital in Oxnard.

I improved the first few days, and then, wham, I was taken down hard. I went comatose whenever my body was raised. The injury had affected the parasympathetic nerves that pump blood from extremities to the heart and brain. My pulse and blood pressure were in the toilet. Time went by slowly. Walt came to the hospital every day after driving home from work. Bob came to see me often. Friends came in and out of my room in a blur. It was hard for me to focus on anything.

Finally, after two months of languishing in the hospital, a

cardiologist implanted a pacemaker in my chest, with wires going to both chambers of the heart. The surgery was long and arduous because the doctor could not find a vein in the left chest area that went down to my heart. After three hours of having wires pulled through my body, the pacemaker was installed on the right side. I knew the second that I was plugged into the pacemaker! Life was back!

In the next few days, I was able to sit up and start rehabilitating. Then I reinjured the spinal cord by somehow moving my neck the wrong way.

A spinal cord surgeon said my neck must be fused immediately, because tests showed there was zilch room between the spinal column and spinal cord, putting me at great risk of total paralysis.

I was taken by ambulance to UCLA Medical Center. That evening, a halo was installed into my head. This contraption had to have been thought up in a torture chamber. It is held in place by four head screws, two into the forehead and two into the back of the head, connected to a round metal object that has metal rods going down to the waist. A straitjacket apparatus kept the rods in place. A pop out button on my chest could be used if I went into cardiac arrest.

An attendant wheeled me to surgery the next morning. C-3 through C-7 was fused with plates and screws.

I was lying in bed on rods that supported the halo around my head when I woke up from sedation. This was horrible. Vision was limited to a little square of the ceiling. Head movement had been cut off. Recuperation was excruciating. My world had shrunk. I had to wear the pisser for two months. Getting around was agonizingly painful and difficult. My neck was torqued backward by the rods secured by this halo contraption, supported by the screws that went into my head.

I was close to being incontinent. The "urine police" were constantly scanning my bladder to see if I was capable of emptying it. This was a hard fight because all feeling had stopped on the left side of my body—it takes patience, concentration, and perseverance to evacuate.

Finally, I was released to go home. It had been three months of hospitalization since the injury. Our next-door neighbor worked for a senior health-care corporation. He scrounged a hospital bed for me to use downstairs in our living room. Walt was again pushing me around in a wheelchair and doing the cooking, as well as making sure I was clean and all my needs were met, in between driving sixty miles to and from work. Bob's help was a blessing, along with that of all our friends.

This entire trauma happened in the middle of the Clinton/Lewinsky sex scandal. I voraciously followed each step of the process on television and talked to Walt and our friends about the political repercussions of having an American president who had lied under oath to a grand jury.

Christmas came, and I was still in the halo. Walt thought it was a swell idea to hang Christmas balls from the halo. I had no humor. My answer was not nice. The dreadful contraption I was trapped in made me feel like my head was blowing up.

On one of our weekly trips to the spinal cord surgeon, I was particularly low in spirit (he torqued my neck back with halo wrenches farther and farther with each visit). This procedure hurt like hell. While I was lying on the office bed, he leaned down over me and said, "You *will* get well!" I smiled back, with tears in my eyes, and said, "Thank you," and felt much better.

After the halo was finally removed, recuperation finally began in earnest. I could not believe how heavy my head was. Rebuilding the muscles in my neck was not effortless. For the next four months my total energy was to learn to make my right hand, arm, and leg move and gain strength. I can't feel my left side. Balance is gone on the right side—boy, do I miss having balance! Handrails needed to be installed on all our steps. I dragged my right leg because I couldn't lift it. I knew I was doomed to a wheelchair if I did not put extreme effort into rehabilitation. Therapists told me any movement and improvement in spinal cord patients had to be made within the first year of an injury. They put me through extreme exercises that made my body begin to respond. I didn't mind the pain, I just wanted to walk and move my non-functioning limbs.

On the first anniversary of my accident, I was walking without a cane and could tie my shoes and feed myself. Three months later, I got up on a water ski. It took lots of patience to help me. Walt had to hold me up from falling over while he tried to make my right foot jam itself into the ski's back binding. The next trick was moving me into the water. I finally figured out that if I just fell sideways into the water, I could drag my ski and legs out into the middle of the river with my arms. Once I had a hold of the ski line, and the line was taut, the boat pulled me up. Right away it was apparent that it took lots of concentration to not fall over. I could move from one side of the wake to the other, but not with my usual exuberance (no extreme cutting or jumping). At the end of my ski run I skied into our beach, fell on my face, and came up with sand between my teeth; however, no one could wipe the smile off my face. Then I tried kayaking. Getting in and out of the kayak was not smooth or graceful, but my paddling technique was unimpaired. It is amazing how weak we become when we can't exercise. The old saying "Use it or lose it" is fact.

|*A river paddle takeoff beach*|

My right hand is numb, stiff, and a lot weaker than my left. If I'm not looking at my right hand, I don't know what it is feeling, doing, or where it is going (I knock glasses out of friends' hands if I lose eye contact with my hand). When I water-ski or kayak, all I ask my right hand to do is to hang onto the ski line or paddle. My arm muscles do the rest. There is little ability to lift my right leg. If a friend gives me a hug and releases me from his or her arms too quickly, I fall, since there is no ability to balance myself on the right side. I can't tell temperature, or if I get hurt on the left side of my body, because I can't feel anything. Walt and I ride our mountain bikes on short, cushy rides. I work out on the elliptical machine, swim laps, or kayak a few miles, do hundreds of squats, stretching exercises, and weight work daily. With the help of hiking sticks, I can hike on uneven terrain, if my crooked toes let me.

Optimal health requires commitment. Restrictive inabilities test my will to push on. I have to have strong muscles to keep upright and not fall over. Throughout my life I ran everywhere. Now, I walk carefully.

9/11 Attack

America, along with the administration of the newly elected president, George W. Bush, was not overly concerned about a terrorist threat to America.

On September 11, 2001, nineteen Muslim jihadist perpetrators (fifteen from Saudi Arabia, two from United Arab Emirates, one from Egypt, and one from Lebanon) flew two American Airlines commercial jets into the World Trade Center towers in New York City, toppling both. They also flew one commercial jet into the Pentagon, and another hijacked commercial jet crashed in Pennsylvania. All four airliners were fully loaded with passengers.

The men were well educated and had successful backgrounds. Mohammad Atta was the lead jihadist. His luggage did not make the connection from his Portland flight. The luggage contained papers that revealed the identity of all nineteen hijackers, their plans, motives, and backgrounds.

On the day of the attacks, the NSA intercepted communications that pointed to the involvement of Osama bin Laden, who had an al-Qaeda training camp in Afghanistan. After complex and extensive investigations, involving over seven thousand special agents, the US government determined that al-Qaeda, headed by Osama bin Laden, bore responsibility for the attacks. The FBI stated that the evidence is clear and irrefutable.

The World Trade Center towers were New York City's most famous structures. Built in the late 1960s, the towers were each 110 stories high. They housed a major portion of downtown Manhattan's business offices. Fifty thousand people worked in the buildings, with another two hundred thousand passing through on a normal workday. Five hundred companies had offices in the complex. At the time of the attack, it was believed that tens of thousands of people could have been trapped inside. Ultimately, 2,749 death certificates were filed.

Ground was broken to build the Pentagon on September 11, 1941, exactly sixty years before it was hit by a hijacked commercial jet. One hundred people working in the hexagon-shaped building were killed.

Walt and I went to Las Vegas to visit friends and celebrate our friend Joyce's birthday a couple of months later. Her boyfriend introduced us to a guy he had met the night before who he said was a sailor. Walt and I thought we were going to meet a "rag sailor." Instead, we met a United States Navy Admiral who was attending a tech-show in Las Vegas. Twenty-six of his people were killed in the Pentagon airliner strike. His office was in the West Wing, where the airplane hit, but he was not on-site and told us he wished he had been because his survival skills could have been useful.

The fourth hijacked plane crashed in a field in Pennsylvania. It was headed for Washington, DC, but the passengers rallied and overtook the hijackers. They were able to stop the plane from continuing on course. The words "let's roll" were heard over a cell phone of one of the passengers. This heroic deed saved another vital American structure from being hit and inflicting more casualties.

The Los Angeles Air Force Base was closed. Heavy cement barriers were placed across all access to the base. The on-base Aerospace Corporation was closed. Walt came home from work and we headed for the river. The FAA halted all flight operations at the nation's airports for the first time in history. Our sky at the river looked quiet and strange. We were used to seeing contrails of jet airliners crisscrossing this very busy skyway to and from Los Angeles.

The US military was put on high alert. Fighter jets were in our skies, ready to shoot down anything that flew. Wall Street closed.

President Bush addressed the nation and vowed to find those responsible and bring them to justice. He pledged a crusade to rid the world of evildoers. Vice President Cheney warned that those who harbor terrorists face the full wrath of the United States. Bush labeled the attacks acts of war and asked Congress for $20 billion to rebuild the destroyed structures.

Secretary of State Colin Powell identified Osama bin Laden as the prime suspect that was responsible for organizing the attack. Fifty thousand reserve troops were called to active duty.

Osama bin Laden issued a tape saying, "Terrorism against America deserved to be praised because it is a response to injustice aimed at forcing America to stop its support of Israel, which kills our people."

The 9/11 Commission report determined that the animosity toward the United States felt by al Qaeda's Khalid Sheikh Mohammed, the principal architect of the 9/11 attacks, stemmed from his violent disagreement with US foreign policy favoring Israel.

The Bush administration said that al-Qaeda was motivated by hatred of the freedom, democracy, and civil liberties exemplified by the United States.

Governments worldwide denounced the 9/11 attacks. France's *Le Monde* newspaper summed up the international mood with the headline: "We Are All Americans." However, reports in the *Wall Street Journal* and the *New York Times* stated that Palestinians celebrated the 9/11 attacks on the United States.

The United States sent a message to Afghanistan to hand over Osama bin Laden or risk massive assault. Taliban leaders called on Muslims to wage holy war on America, if it attacked. The Pentagon ordered combat aircraft to the Persian Gulf. Saudi Arabia cut ties with the Taliban government.

President Bush spoke from the pile of rubble at the World Trade Center site. With his arm around a fireman who was part of the ongoing rescue effort, he told Americans that we would get bin Laden and the al-Qaeda terrorists. America was not asked to sacrifice. This war was to be fought using volunteer forces and not reinstituting the draft, as we had in World War II and the Korean and Vietnam wars.

The people of America supported Bush and were solidly behind his decision to invade Afghanistan, wipe out al-Qaeda and the Taliban, and get bin Laden. It was one of the few times in our nation's history that we pulled together for a military invasion.

The Federal Reserve cut interest rates in hopes of keeping the economy from faltering. The stock market plunged on the first day of trading after the attacks. We watched our retirement funds whither.

In early October 2001, President Bush ordered the invasion of Afghanistan to overthrow the Taliban and attempt to destroy al-Qaeda. International support was generously given to back America in its quest to extirpate the enemy.

If Afghanistan's leaders had turned over bin Laden and his al-Qaeda network, an invasion could have been averted.

Afghanistan was quickly taken over by international military forces, led by US General Tommy Franks. Al-Qaeda leaders, including bin Laden, were forced into the mountains of Tora-Bora. Franks decided not to pursue them. Bin Laden and al-Qaeda leaders escaped over the mountains into Pakistan, where bin Laden was found and killed ten years later.

Bush pursued an invasion into Iraq in 2003. Many statesmen and political leaders within our own country were not convinced America needed to invade a country that was not a threat and had no known connection with 9/11.

The Bush Doctrine: "The National Security Strategy of Pre-emptive Strikes" comes under the UN Charter, which gives the right of self-defense to every country.

The case to invade Iraq was built on the belief that Iraq's leader, Saddam Hussein, possessed WMD and would use them to attack the United States.

Vice President Cheney was well respected and knowledgeable regarding the Middle East. Most Americans, including me, thought there was justifiable cause to invade Iraq because of what we were being told.

In February of 2003, Secretary of State Colin Powell went before the United Nations and staked his credibility on firsthand descriptions of biological weapons on wheels and that Iraq had a huge stockpile of WMDs and was determined to acquire nuclear weapons. He stated there was a link between al-Qaeda and Iraq.

Powell had questions about what he said—the official information given him had come from an old and outdated National Intelligence Estimate that was disregarded by the intelligence community because of innuendoes instead of facts.

The international community was not convinced of the need to invade Iraq. Daily newspapers described how wrong other nations felt America was to go to war in Iraq. Great Britain's Prime Minister Tony Blair was the only world leader to fully support the US invasion strategy. The people of Great Britain were opposed to the invasion. In the run-up to war, the WMD scenario was pursued. The UN's chief weapons of mass-destruction investigator was David Kay. He was checking Iraqi sites off the list, one after another, but found no smoking gun.

America changed after 9/11. The security of airports and government agencies went to Code Red. Protecting the United States of America from terrorist attack was the primary goal for our military and law enforcement agencies.

The military and civilian leaders in the Pentagon were at loggerheads on the strategy of how to invade Iraq. Secretary of Defense Donald Rumsfeld led the charge for an invasion focused on air power. It had worked in the Gulf War. He did not see the need for a large number of troops on the ground, even though many military leaders were saying hundreds of thousands of troops would be needed.

Military leaders were also questioning the rationale of invading a Middle Eastern country that was not a threat to us. Where was the plan for postinvasion? War planning to invade Iraq was all we heard on news networks and in newspapers.

Our troops quickly toppled Saddam Hussain, capturing him. He was tried before an Iraqi court. Saddam was convicted of heinous crimes and hung. By this time a civil war between the Sunni and Shiite factions ensued. They are still fighting, but the Shiites took control of their government. We exited Iraq in 2011.

Barack Obama, a black man with an Islamic name, was elected president in 2008, amid a financial collapse of our banking system. The Iraq and Afghanistan wars ended under his two terms in office.

Mental war fatigue had taken a toll on us. The solution— change venues.

Sojourn to the Rockies

Walt took a work transfer back to Colorado Springs, Colorado. The project centered between Peterson Air Force Base, contractor locations, and the Aerospace facility.

After settling into our new apartment on Cheyenne Mountain, I had our little Toyota truck packed with camping gear most every Friday afternoon when Walt came home from work. We headed for the Rocky Mountains.

Colorado is mile-high country, with fifty-two peaks soaring more than fourteen thousand feet above sea level.

About half of Colorado lies within the Rockies. The backbone of Colorado's High Country forms part of the Continental Divide.

Accumulated waters, flowing to the east, reach the Gulf of Mexico by way of the Arkansas, the South Platte, and the Rio Grande rivers.

Drainage to the west, which eventually reaches the Pacific Ocean, is through the Colorado River system flowing from the Continental Divide, gathering speed and snowmelt, then converging with the Green River below Moab, Utah. The hydroelectric dams in the river's path provide electricity to millions. Cities such as Las Vegas draw their water supply from Lake Meade. When it gets to our river house, the farmers use it for growing their crops. Phoenix, Los Angeles, and Mexico get a portion of their water from the Colorado River.

Geologically, the Rocky Mountain chain is young—sixty to seventy million years old. Slow, intermittent movements of the earth's crust produced the folding and buckling that raised the bedrock gradually, over time, to those lofty heights. Glaciers, during the last three ice ages, sculpted many of the peaks into the sharp, jagged shapes of today.

For all of its outward ruggedness, the Rockies are delicate country. Many of the roads and trails lead far above tree line and into the strange and beautiful world of alpine tundra. The display of wildflowers in the summer is spectacular. Ridge after ridge of mountain ranges, far into the distance, and in all directions, with glacial lakes below, is a feast for hikers' eyes.

Summer storms move in by early afternoon, which can be gentle and short, or severe and violent, and last all night. We learned the hard way to put up our tent and a protective tarp outside the tent as quickly as possible when we arrived at a campsite.

When the weather turned bad, we ate peanuts and shared some with the wildlife, drank a little wine, and watched the rain and lightning, while Walt competed with the thunder playing his banjo or guitar.

One of our favorite mountain areas to camp and explore is Crested Butte. This is a great place to hike in the summer. On one of our weekend camping trips to this resort area, we pitched our tent in a field of clover and built a fire. The next morning we drove up a winding dirt road to a lodge in the mountains above Crested Butte.

I had left my hiking sticks at our campsite. After visiting the lodge, we spotted a path and started to explore where it took us. The trail went straight up. I looked for a piece of wood that would work as a hiking stick, Pretty soon we were above timber line, and I knew I would be stick-less coming down the mountain. Walking downhill or on uneven terrain is difficult with my lack of balance on the right side. Hanging onto Walt was my only option.

We climbed to an escarpment that overlooked snow-covered peaks. Fragile tundra was the sole plant life at this altitude. The dramatic beauty made us feel giddy.

We met another couple standing on the overlook. The woman warned us to not step on the fragile plant life. I told her this was difficult for me because I had no control over where I might step, but I would do my best to avoid the little green plants. Upon hearing my problem, the woman offered me her hiking sticks. I enthusiastically accepted her offer, and we arranged to leave the sticks in the bar of the lodge we had passed.

I had no problem going downhill and did not step on any flora or fauna. When we reached the lodge, we saw a large outside balcony that overlooks a lake. We bought a beer (Colorado's Fat Tire beer) and set on top of the railing to drink our brew. While we were basking in the sun and generally enjoying life, the couple we had met on top of the mountain came by. I expressed my appreciation of having hiking sticks to get me downhill. We bought the couple a beer. A new friendship was born.

In southcentral Colorado, the 12,120-foot-high Cottonwood Pass crosses the Continental Divide. Cottonwood Campground is the take-off point for a hiking trail that goes to the top of Brown's Pass. We camped by a stream, close to where the hike begins. It's a strenuous uphill hike to the top, but the rewards are great. The raw beauty is boldly displayed—wildflowers cover the ground under a pristine-blue Colorado sky. The surrounding white pinnacles of the fourteen-thousand-foot Collegiate Peaks look like you could reach out and touch them. This is a special place. Few people make the climb.[6]

Twin Lakes, two of the deepest and largest lakes in the Rockies, lies below Mount Elbert. We camped near the Roaring Fork River and hiked up and around the mountain—didn't make it to the top, but what a view!

Pikes Peak, at 14,110 feet, is visible from most anywhere in Colorado Springs. Southwest of the peak, along a rocky little stream known as Cripple Creek, lies one of the most famous gold fields in the world. A worthless-looking six-square-mile grassy plateau in the crater of an extinct volcano has yielded more gold than any other single deposit ever found.

---

6   When Walt's father, Jack, passed away he was cremated. We hiked to this same overlook, with Jack's ashes in Walt's backpack, and placed his remains on a rock that overlooks the Taylor River—far below our vantage point. Trout fishing on the Taylor River was Jack's favorite relaxation. His ashes were whisked away in a gentle mountain breeze.

|Hiking up Colorado's Brown's Pass to where the Continental Divide is within striking distance|

The Colorado Trail snakes its way across the Rockies from Durango northward to Denver. It connects more than five hundred miles of mountains, crossing eight ranges, seven national forests, six wilderness areas, and the headwaters of five river systems. The trail winds though rugged high terrain and pristine meadows. Most of the trail is above ten thousand feet. The highest point is 13,334 feet. Wildflowers change with the ascent. Vistas open to panoramas that are breathtaking. It was a thrill to hike part of this trail!

Rocky Mountain National Park is in northern Colorado, where the Continental Divide crosses the park. The Colorado River begins its journey from here. Walt and I hiked up into the headwaters and watched the river trickle through ice and snow on its quest southward. We stepped across the nascent stream in a giant stride. The mighty Colorado picks up steam as it roars down through the western slopes of the Rockies.

Hiking along the top of a 12,500-foot mountain, where the wind howls and little plants have developed hair on their leaves to keep warm, was a study in keeping your feet firmly planted on the rocky terrain. The roots of these fragile plants go as far as five feet underground, even though the plants are no more than an eighth of an inch high. Snow blows in drifts and rarely covers the ground at the peak of the mountain because the wind doesn't let the snow accumulate.

The tundra in this high country is an island of arctic vegetation. Other small plants called lichen cling to rocks, getting their nourishment from the minerals in the rock, and eventually breaking the rocks.

We climbed on volcanic boulders, took in the breathtaking view, and had to hug each other because we felt so blessed.

|*View from Rocky Mountain National Park's apex*|:

That evening was spent in a log cabin B&B at the bottom of the mountain. It had a hot tub right in the middle of an aspen forest. A glass of wine put the finishing touch on a perfect day as we viewed the sunset while relaxing our tired bodies, letting the bubbles blast our tight muscles.

Return to the Beach from Colorado

Winter was just around the corner, and being the fun-in-the-sun seekers we are, it was time to head back to sun-drenched California. Aerospace again came to the rescue! They transferred

Walt back to a different program within their Los Angeles Air Force Base location.

Before leaving Colorado in November, my goal to snow ski again was fulfilled. It was a triumph! Our Colorado friends Hank and Sylvia went with us to Keystone Ski Resort for the weekend. The ski shop comped my skis, poles, and boots when they learned that I placed third in the fifty and over women's age category in the Ironman Triathlon and had recently suffered a spinal cord injury.

Walt was apprehensive about me getting on the ski lift and asked me to stay on the bunny slopes. Only the higher-elevation steeper slopes were open. Besides, Hank and Sylvia (who are expert skiers), were there to pick me up when I fell and "bird-dog" me down the hill.

I did not ski anything like I did before the injury (I must have fallen a hundred times in the snow because I couldn't edge with my right ski), but I felt darned good about my effort. That evening we soaked ourselves in the hot water of the Keystone Lodge Jacuzzi and rolled in the snow, laughing and celebrating heartily!

The movers gathered up our belongings at our apartment in Colorado Springs, and we took off in our SUV and headed west to our home in warm and wonderful Southern California.

Living next to the beach, watching sailboats tack to weather from the sandy shoreline, with the Channel Islands off in the distance, is the ultimate picturesque setting. Sailing to Santa Cruz Island for the weekend is an adventure never to be missed. Playing in the desert is an ideal contrast.

Afterword

The impact that sailing has had on my life is enormous. Walt wrote the following poem to me after a particularly exhilarating day of sailboat racing aboard *Vanishing Girl* with Bob at the helm. The three of us, and the rest of the crew, celebrated a win.

The Essence of Life

Thinking of you riding with me, in the spume and spray
Reaching out, close hauled, far from shore and quay
An inauguration! A wonderful place to begin
The foam, feather'd arrow to where we've been.

The sails are solid, formed, and well set.
The bow greets each swell, and, in turn, is met.
Surfing each wave as it comes along
With you in my heart, my life, my soul's song!

Take another turn on the winch, tie the line off!
On the rail over the deep, we smile and then scoff

As we fly, pursued, pursuing the dolphins in the blue.
With the main trim'd, we await the captain's cue.

The maestro's on the helm watching for every turn.
Watching, searching the horizon, feeling the wind's burn!
And what of these poor souls shackled to the shore?
Unbaptized by spray and spume, without the ocean's roar.

On starboard tack, near the windward mark,
The foredeck man and the crew await the master's bark.
Now! And the chute goes up hand over hand
"And down with the foresail" is his next command.

The spinnaker's full, set wide and true;
The vang, the outhaul's released, so's the clew.
With a whisper 'pon the wave, upon the foam,
With you in my arms I feel at home!

The pure happiness achieved in an exhilarating sailing race is hard to explain to landlubbers. Going to weather in a twenty-five-knot breeze and big seas is a hang-onto-your-britches exciting adventure. Looking up to the top of the mast, groaning under the stress put on the rigging, I hoped and prayed the boat held together. If we beat our competition to the weather mark, the spinnaker set was crucial to maintaining our lead. If we were playing catch-up, the spinnaker set was just as crucial. Our goal was to blanket the boat in front and steal his wind.

Battling our way to the finish line always created anxiety. Everyone on the boat focused on their job, trying desperately to get every ounce of speed out of our boat as it surfed its way across the waves.

The race is over—we crossed the finish line. High-fives are given—cold beer is brought out from down below. Happiness, success, and pride—exuberant bear hugs between our close-knit fellow sailors, who can't wipe the smiles from their sun-burned faces.

Planning, preparation, and hard work took us to our achieved goal of doing well or winning the race.

Goin' to weather is a lifetime objective.

We must never stop trying our best to sail hard and fast through headwinds. A creative mind and a healthy body want to be exercised. Drive and determination, channeled toward worthy goals, are the ingredients of success.

Keen perception brings goals into focus. Sedulous attention to those goals brings progress to attainment. Enthusiasm brings happiness and fulfillment.

"He who is of a calm and happy nature will hardly feel the pressure of age and time, but to him who is of an opposite disposition, youth and age are equally a heavy burden."
—Plato, *The Republic*

Without the above ingredients, life would cease to be special. Therefore, a consequential life never stops pursuing great efforts to grow to new heights.

"I am the master of my fate,
I am the captain of my soul."
—William Ernest Henley's "Invictus"

Today's world is both exciting and uncertain. I revel in its complexity.

Life is sweet.

|A Sunday morning Jacuzzi soak after a kayak paddle|

About the Author

Sally Bond was born in Iowa in the middle of the Depression and grew up with midwestern family values. After she moved to California in her late teens, she embraced a more adventuresome lifestyle that includes sailing, triathlons, mountain biking, and kayaking. She currently lives in California.

Bibliography

Brzezinski, Zbiggniew. *Second Chance: Three Presidents and the Crisis of American Superpower.* New York: Basic Books, 2007

Encyclopedia Britannica, Inc. *The New Encyclopedia Britannica Volume 15: Knowledge In Depth.*. University of Chicago, 1992.

Frankl, Viktor. *Man's Search For Meaning: An introduction to Logotherapy.* New York: Buccaneer, 1959

Hemingway, Ernest. *For Whom The Bell Tolls.* New York: MacMillan, 1940

Henley, William. *Invictus: poem:* the Art of Manliness. 1861. Bibliographic Record: *Modern British Poetry,* Louis Untermeyer. New York: Harcort, 1920.

Kennedy, David. *Freedom From Fear: the American People in Depression and War, 1929–1945* New York: Oxford University, 1999.

Lama, Dalai. The Art of Happiness: a Handbook for Living. New York; Penguin, 1998.

Maslow, Abraham. *Toward a Psychology of Being: Humanistic Psychology.* New York: D. Van Nostrand, 1968.

National Commission Members. *9/11 Commission Report: Terrorist Attacks upon the United States.* New York: W. W. Norton, 2006.

Plato. *The Republic: Philosophy.*300 BC. *A New Translation,* Christopher Rowe. United Kingdom: Penguin, 2012.

Teeple, John. *Timelines of World History: a Chronicle of Human History.* New York: Dorling Kindersley, 2006.

Woodward, Bob. *The War Within: A Secret White House History 2006-2008. New York: Simon & Schuster,* 2008.